Behind and Beyond the Letters
by
Cliff Slade
ISBN: 978-1-9164271-6-7

2

Published by

i2i
PUBLISHING

i2i Publishing
Manchester. UK
www.i2ipublishing.co.uk

People who know me will realise how much they don't know me and people who don't know me will realise how much they do know me. The only person who truly knows me is Julie, my wife.

This book is dedicated to Julie, my wife.

Foreword

I started writing a few letters to my weekly local newspaper, *The Tenbury Advertiser*, and people said to me that they liked my letters. Some said, 'what a load of rubbish!'; others remarked on how they looked forward to my letters, and it wasn't the same if I didn't have one printed that week. Many people said that they scanned the letters column and, if my name wasn't there, they didn't bother reading the others. They even said how it cheered them up and how funny or how right I was.

One morning, while I was shopping around Tenbury, four separate people, within the space of an hour, said, 'I hope you are keeping all these letters and putting them in a book', 'You should write a book', 'I love your letters' and 'I'm looking forward to next week to feel uplifted and feel good after reading another one of your letters'. Now isn't that strange, and why do people engage with my short observations and truthful musings on a particular theme or topic?

Isn't it strange that with fashion, academia, theories, wars, writing styles, writers, and even the incredible evolution in communication technology, the humble letter is still as apparent and important today as it was when scribes first etched their manuscripts?

Isn't it strange, how a letter in the twenty first century can now be received in the form of an email or a text message, Facebook, or through the post via the Royal Mail, and still survive and change throughout the test of time?

Isn't it strange that a letter can be a love exchange, or a weapon of hate, a protest, apology, confession, complaint, compliment, conciliation, pacification, aggression, politics, religion, hello, goodbye, regret, hope, or despair?

Isn't it strange how a letter defines, identifies or hides the author's character, agenda, class, personality, integrity, charm, disposition, creed, colour, culture, intelligence and well-being?

Isn't it strange that throughout my childhood and formative years, a framed, abridged and altered version of a poem on my wall within our family home meant so much to me and was framing and forming my own character, just by reading it every day? Its subliminal message was mirroring my own account of life:

> Princes & Kings
> Isn't it strange that princes and kings,
> and clowns that caper in sawdust rings,
> and ordinary folk, like you and me,
> are builders of eternity?
>
> Each are given a set of rules;
> an hour glass and a bag of tools.
> And each must build, 'ere life is flown,
> A stumbling block, or a stepping-stone.
>
> R. L. Sharpe

I am one of the ordinary builder folk and allowed myself to be a beginner. I realised and accepted that I did not start out perfect or excellent but believed in myself to grow and develop to be the best I can be, and I am!

I have lived and experienced, but most of all, have learnt during life's events that my character and beliefs, through my connection and relationship with loved ones, family, friends, colleagues and acquaintances, have caused me, at times, to trip, but also to get up and move forward with a new awareness and appreciation of others' views and opinions, with empathy, congruence and positive regard.

I want to share with you some of those letters and share my thoughts beyond the letter. I also want to write some new letters to you and others. I want this to be a book of letters about letters and about me, who and why I am what I am, and maybe you will see a bit of you in me.

Yours sincerely
Kind regards
Yours faithfully
Yours truly
Best wishes
Sincerely yours

Cliff Slade
Tenbury Wells

Preface

This book is a book written in letters. These letters were printed in the local media or written by the author to himself or his family. Inspired by a seemingly invisible love story between a husband and his wife, and a love for his family, these letters take us through an unstoppable journey of 'rags to riches', not only financially, but more importantly, emotionally.

As well as a local, social and political commentary, these letters and musings are an inspirational handbook about how a working-class lad from a one-parent 1960s family made a success of his life, emotionally, spiritually and mentally because he 'felt the fear' and did it anyway, and believed, 'whatever the mind can conceive and believe, it can achieve'. Sometimes sad, sometimes amusing, sometimes painful but always meaningful, true and progressive, this is a letter of love and affection, and a touching personal, emotional victory and accomplishment.

Cliff Slade

Acknowledgements

Simon Whaley for being the first to read my manuscript and never suggesting I change anything, whilst sharing with me his views, observations, and experience as an accomplished writer and author. Thank you to him for reading and comprehensively responding to all those emails I sent to him. He really is a genuine, helpful, good person.

Lionel Ross, my publisher, for untiringly allowing me to be rude to him and tolerating me as I regularly interrogated him and tried to understand the publishing industry. Thank you to him and his team, including Gemma, my editor, for all their hard work in producing my book.

My sister, Pauline, for reading my raw manuscript and understanding and accepting this was my story. Finally, my mum, for all the unceasing hard work and dedication that being a mum demands.

Book Cover: Design by Matt Maguire

No Particular Place to Start but a Particular and Strong Feeling

One of my town's local councillors appeared on the front-page headline of my local newspaper, in picture and in print, debasing my town, Tenbury Wells and its people, which included me as a resident. His piece basically stated that we were all generally apathetic, and the whole town was petering and slipping into a coma, and the people were doomed for a future of dreariness. All his ranting was because a venue could not be found for his boxing club and an upcoming boxing night, for which the tickets weren't particularly selling well.

So, I wrote this, and it went into print. I received a great deal of positive and supportive feedback; readers really liked it. So why did I write it, and why did people like it?

Cliff Slade has written this response to last week's front-page story in The Tenbury Advertiser, in which a councillor said Tenbury had lost its heart after struggling to find a new venue for the boxing club he founded.

Hey Councillor – I'm going to have to 'put my gloves on and take you on' for this one! Our town's spirit is far from broken. I am around the town most days and certainly, every morning, collecting my daily newspaper at Tenbury News, or a local supermarket. I have a great laugh almost every day, not only with the staff, but also with the local people. Spirits certainly seem very high.

I also regularly walk through the town in the evening and just feel what a great place it is to be. Walking past the Regal is a joy when it is all lit up. It looks brilliant and that is before you enter the theatre to see a local production, or a national, or upcoming top act, or even a night at the flicks to watch a top film at this newly-refurbished venue.

A couple of evenings ago, I went to The Talbot, another local newly-refurbished venue, and had a first-class meal. This new, top-class eatery complements Tenbury's already top-notch restaurants such as The Pembroke, Rose and Crown, Peacock, Ship and Fountain, to name but a few.

If you want to see a live band every weekend, just pop into The Bridge where young and old mix within a vibrant, happy, relaxed atmosphere, and it really is quite an uplifting place to be. Furthermore, in the evening, whether you just fancy an Indian meal, or a Chinese meal, or even a kebab, or pizza, Tenbury really has everything to offer.

In the day, if you just fancy a cuppa and a sarnie, or even something more sophisticated, walk into Tabs, Spotty Dog, or The Tav, where upon plentiful supply of spirit and life are apparent.

I also walked past Cafe 27, and that was overspilling with youngsters laughing and joking. I crossed the road down the side of our brilliant town library, where the writers' group and choir meet.

I then passed our tennis club and bowling club, crossing our children's playground, then past our snooker club, who are finalists in the club leagues – so plenty of spirit there too.

I then entered the Palmers' Meadow where every weekend plenty of sporting spirit is apparent from our football teams and rugby team, where again young junior teams and first senior teams are all well represented.

After supporting or playing in any of the teams, you can walk over to our fantastic swimming pool and cool down, or even aspire to be like our local sportsmen and build up some muscle in the gym.

Councillor, take a walk around our local brilliant junior and senior schools with inspiring teachers, and just as important, some fantastic well-motivated and spirited students, who year after year, exceed expectations in exam results. This is where spirit and energy is more than obvious.

We have so many well-supported organisations, which time and again, give to our community, like the Freemasons, The British Legion, The Round Table, W.I. and Tenbury Town Band. You will not find 'low ebbs' in these groups.

We have a fire station manned by local volunteers. We have a hospital, a doctors' surgery and a couple of dentists, a post office and two of the best taxi companies in the region. We have some great local shops that were here long before me. Yes, we have lost some, but we also have new ones.

We have both major and minor industries which employ a great deal of people. Our local, district and county councillors and MPs are fighting our corner.

Councillor, don't judge our townsfolk's mood and our destiny on boxing tickets not selling well, or finding a new boxing club venue.

Pick yourself up, brush yourself down, and look at our positives.

My old boxing trainer, who is still about, was Bengi Brittain.

He always told me to punch, roll and move. Hey Councillor - if I were your 'corner man', I would be trying to lift you and motivate you, and get the best from you, even if the going gets tough. Look up, keep your chin up, change tactic.

I may even spray a bit of magic water on your face.

As my local councillor, I expect the same from you. Talk our town and its people up, look at what we have, and just what a successful high-spirited place this town really is. I, for one, could not think of a better spirited place to live.

CLIFF SLADE
Tenbury Wells

I was surprised that this letter was printed because as letters go in local newspapers, it was rather long, but why did I write it, and how?

I certainly penned it very quickly and found it very easy to construct. This particular councillor is not so local, and a guy who suddenly appeared as a co-opted councillor (so, not even elected), and also happened, for the last five minutes, to run a boxing club in one of our pubs in the town. He was a good-looking lad, a dapper dresser and apparently a decent boxer. He flounced about in his over-large car, and his confidence outside of the ring was growing within the community as he had also just been initiated into the local Masonic lodge. However, all three were very short-lived, and in five minutes the boxing club had gone. He was no longer a councillor, nor a Mason. Jab, jab – gone!

I think my tone in the previous paragraph certainly gives an insight into my own character, and at least the reasoning for just replying to the headline story produced in his name. It was not this particular guy's fault that I was blunt with my observations of him; it was just my perception and transference of feelings or emotions that I had, negatively or positively, gathered from others along my way.

I was brought up on a council estate and was very shy, introverted and went through infant and primary school without speaking to a teacher. Apparently, I would have been classed as a mute today. Although I didn't speak, I was a great listener – good job really or I would have been classed as both bloody deaf *and* dumb! So, individuals being confident and extroverted, in dapper wear, flouncing about in fancy cars push a few buttons with me. This, coupled with the fact that this person could easily have beaten me up and that he was better looking than me, reached far back to a primal instinct.

Tenbury Wells has been good to me. I moved to Tenbury when I was fifteen in 1975 from Worcester, so it was a big shock from a city to a town of four thousand people. I went to school for six months at Tenbury Comprehensive School. I have some good friends from those days. I met my wife in Tenbury. I brought up my children in Tenbury and immersed myself in the town – a town and people I have come to love. So, when someone rubbishes my place when they are temporarily breezing through, and I have feelings for it, a response is invariably provoked.

I could go deeper and write a psychology book on why I wrote one letter. However, I think including other letters that I have penned, will show other reasoning and analytical interpretations with which we may both associate life experiences.

So, isn't it strange, that reading a headlined article stirred up such a personal and emotional response within me, resulting in my lettered response?

The rest of the letter was pretty easy and straight forward. I just imagined myself walking around my town, passing its amenities, places and clubs etc. which gave the letter a pace and rhythm. Finally, I played on the boxing and boxer analogies, which gave the letter a pace with a sprinkle of humour.

Why did it appeal to other people (the readers) when it was just my view and interpretation based on my life experiences? Was it the fight? Was it being proud of Tenbury? Was it the rhythm? Was it the humour, or do we all have the same experiences and emotions? I doubt it! Was the letter positive on the back of a negative? Was it uplifting?

In this councillor's defence, he was interviewed, and it was the journalist who wrote the article, which opens up a completely different agenda and game play. The bottom line is that the journalist got a response from me, which gave his article further mileage! I know the councillor remonstrated and remarked around town about his article and my response and that he was misquoted and not happy. As I don't suffer fools lightly – 'Hey Councillor, write it yourself next time!'

***

In the beginning...

I do not want to write or go through a self-therapy experience, but it is a fact that the way we conduct our lives, and the way in which we behave with others, are based on our learnt behaviour from our parents or significant others. Therefore, I have to regress and include some of my childhood experiences and events to link in with the way I, or you, may write or communicate today.

Briefly, I mentioned that I was brought up on a council estate and I was very shy, painfully self-conscious and never interacted with my teachers, albeit, I did have lots of friends and was able to develop and interact normally with them (whatever 'normal' means!). I also was a great listener, but because I didn't interact with my teachers, I was, most of the time, having to listen carefully to work matters out myself. This, coupled with no father figure in my life, presented challenges for me, inasmuch as, no one showed me how to do things. For the record, my parents split and divorced when I was around five. Why didn't my mother show me how to do things? Probably because she was busy bringing up a family of three, soon-to-be four, as a single parent in the early sixties, and in her generation the father did the practical and life lessons in life, and the mother mothered and cooked. So, having to listen, and not having the confidence or encouragement to communicate, I had to adopt a strategy in life to be heard and seen – to be somebody.

With today's psychological and specially trained teachers and social care teams on hand in schools, I would have been identified as special needs, with all the support that would attract, but this was the sixties! However, being a great listener and having to work things out myself gave me a massive advantage, as I really did adopt an ability to work things out quickly.

Later in life, as a fire fighter during some training, a phrase was introduced which exactly summed up one of my adopted strategies and said everything I was able to do naturally – 'dynamic risk assessment'! I recognised this phrase and its meaning as an everyday character trait that I was blessed to have: to 'act and think dynamically'. I could, within a nanosecond, weigh up people, have an opinion, make a decision, say the right thing, connect, read a protracted and intensive story or report, and have an immediate balanced plan of action. I knew what to say, when to say it, and how to say it, which was, later in life, an asset to enable me to succeed in relationships, management, and in my own business.

Closely associated with my ability to dynamically function, is the fact that I rarely look back, rarely look forward, but I am always living in the very 'now'. Living in the now really is living dynamically. Here is a letter that again, was printed in my local paper, which included me being unusually sentimental about the past, but it fitted and was true of my feeling at that moment.

CLIFF SLADE IS FULL OF PRAISE FOR THE ROUND TABLE BONFIRE IN TENBURY

On the evening of the fifth of November, my wife and son attended the Round Table bonfire and firework display at the Burgage in Tenbury.

While walking through Tenbury, we joined the thickening pavements with people also en route to the display.

I couldn't help reminiscing, how twenty years earlier, I was also treading the same path – albeit, my son was probably riding on my shoulder, whereas today as a twenty-two-year-old, he was now walking taller than me – but we all still had the same exciting anticipation of a great Guy Fawkes evening Tenbury and the Round Table were about to present.

When we arrived, the bonfire was well alight, and the atmosphere and tradition of the occasion was clear to see on the smiles and looks of joy on both children and adults' faces alike.

At this stage, twenty years ago, I would probably have lit a sparkler for my son but this evening he turned around to me and said: 'Do you want a pint, Dad?'

I, again, reflected and considered how things had changed from me lighting his sparkler to him now offering to buy his dad a pint. However, I was quickly returned to reality when he said: 'Can I have some money, then?' Many, many hundreds of people attended this evening, and as well as a fantastic spectacle, it was also a great town, social gathering.

Tenbury Town Band was brilliant, as usual, the hot dogs, burgers etc by Phil Gibbs were delicious, the Scouts' soup kitchen was yummy, and youngsters were happily sliding down a huge inflatable slide.

The organisation was brilliant. £5 to get in was remarkable and once the fireworks started, anyone who was there would agree that it was nothing short of exceptional – a great display enjoyed by all.

My daughter is expecting our first grandchild next month, and I hope that, next year, I will be bringing him or her to the Tenbury Round Table firework display and for many years thereafter. Who knows, they may even pay for Grandad's pint!

A great deal of hard work and effort
must have gone into the organisation and
planning of this occasion, so, a sincere
'thank you' and a 'very well done'.

Not only for this year's excellent
display but for the many past and hopefully, many more years of enjoyment, Tenbury
Round Table has delivered on Guy Fawkes
night. Well done!

CLIFF SLADE
Tenbury Wells

I was really driven to write this letter because of
how truly grateful and appreciative I was of someone
or some organisation's effort, hard work and commitment, for absolutely no reward, other than whatever
drives volunteers to volunteer. All I wanted to say was
'thank you' and 'well done' because the display was
fantastic, but that would be humdrum, brief and unin-
spiring to read so I wrote from the way I live in the
'here and now', at that moment, how I felt from that
dynamic moment. Being able to appreciate and be appreciative and grateful are also huge and important in-
gredients in my character – being thankful is an attraction that attracts.

Anyone at that display must have thought the same
as me that evening and how thankful they were, but isn't
it strange how we infrequently say 'thank you', although,

generally, we so often are thankful? I'm sure the reason people enjoyed this letter was because that is exactly how they felt too, but all too often we leave it to someone else to be grateful on our behalf.

A letter is a little story and has to have a bit of pace. This was introduced again as I was walking down to the display reminiscing. I had a bit of poetic licence to join things together, and a sprinkle of humour, again, to bring a smile, and the whole thing uplifted and made me, the reader, and the organisers feel good.

A couple of the organisers personally thanked me and said it really meant a lot to them.

Being brought up from a humble background, in a one-parent family, when money was tight and our clothes were either hand-knitted or on the never-never, we would rarely have treats other than Crimbo or birthdays, so I was always very grateful, appreciative, and always taught to say thank you. So again, this was a little, but such an important part, of my character being exercised.

This sounds so old-fashioned, but it's so true, and even saying it sounds unbelievable, but when I was around five or six, my old chap was a member of a working men's club in Worcester called 'Rainbow Hill'. Every year they would have a Christmas party where Father Christmas would pay us a visit. It really was the real Father Christmas, honest! He would give us an orange, an apple and a half-crown, and the feeling was incredible. It was as if I had won the lottery and that orange and apple were the best tasting fruit I had ever eaten! I was so appreciative and thankful. I can't ever remember spending the half-crown though. I reckon it went in the gas meter for our home Christmas dinner! Christmas dinner was a cockerel, a big cock; mother always had a big cock at Christmas!

This is another letter, similar and in the same format, that was printed giving sincere thanks again, and was very well received by the organisers.

Dear Editor,
    In past years, I put all my efforts into making shapes in the 'mosh pit' at the brilliant Tenbury Music Festival, to the extent, I am always a little jaded and need recovery time thereafter! My recovery period usually clashed with the following 'Tenbury Party in the Park' event and I have never made it to the party in the park.
    However, this year my two little grandchildren had Sunday roast with us, and we all decided to give it a go. After divesting my bank account at the cash point in anticipation for a costly, summer, family afternoon, we walked in between the swimming pool and the scout hut and 'Wow!' The party in the park hit us

right between the eyes. It really was a party in the park; it was absolutely buzzing with children thoroughly enjoying themselves across most of the Palmer's Meadow.

All the favourite children's entertainments, as well as various local groups, were all comprehensively in place and being enjoyed in full by literally hundreds of families. Similarly, I think every canine in the town and area was also in attendance and in competition with each other. The various dog contests and shows were amazing, with pets groomed, trained and performing to an incredibly high standard.

Such an event doesn't happen by accident, and must have taken a great deal of cost, time and effort to bring together in such an organised and wide-ranging manner. What a fantastic community and family event this was! Apart from a cup of tea and an ice cream, the whole event was free and fully funded by sponsors and volunteers, which was very much appreciated. On behalf of every parent, carer and grandparent who thoroughly enjoyed the afternoon, may I take this opportunity to offer a great big thanks to the organisers, Tenbury Wells' local policing team, and all the sponsors and volunteers for a great

afternoon of entertainment and fun whilst
bringing the community together.

Cliff Slade
Tenbury Wells

With the couple of letters thus far, it is easy to see a format developing, and this can become predictable and less attractive to a letter editor! I'm saying 'thank you'. It's a bit amusing, and we may or may not feel uplifted. I must say that I am aware of letter editors' agenda for printing my letters, and I have had many letters not printed, so being topical, local and different is at the back of my mind, but overall, I can honestly say that I have to be inspired to write a letter, and whether it's printed or not is immaterial to me.

The next letter didn't make the grade or other incoming letters to the editor took precedence at that time, and this didn't go to print. It may have been a bit too cheeky or fruity!

In the media were a lot of food related articles that I had been reading and I thought and thought whilst regressing to my past eating. The professional and social advice being recommended was now turning full circle and contradicting itself – how strange! This letter is a bit serious, but still fosters a smile at the end. Humour, how strange, but just like the poem on my wall, we can all input and make a difference, even clowns!

MIXED FOOD MESSAGES

So many mixed messages and contradictory laboratory studies are confusing me! As a child, any home fried food was cooked in lard, with bread and dripping a welcome bonus! This was considered unhealthy and a heart disease risk, and we were then scared into switching to cooking oils such as vegetable oils. These oils are now considered carcinogenic, and we are now informed that lard is a healthy option. Great!

The Food Standards Agency now informs me over-cooked roast potatoes, chips, crisps and toast can produce acrylamide which causes cancer. Crikey!

As kids, we would choose and fight over the crispiest, darkest roast potato stuck to the roasting pan. Similarly, my toast would be dark and very much well done! Excellent!

The Government's new 'Go for Gold' healthy food campaign now informs me to drop the dark and go for blonde! Whilst studying this advice, I looked across to my wife who is olive-skinned and brunette, and wondered, is she possibly a hazard to my health? Mmmmm!

Being in the twilight of my fifties, the study that really engaged me, was the fact the over-fifties, enjoy and are experiencing the best ever intimate moments compared to any other age group! Wahey!

Putting all the confusing food advice aside, I focused on the good and popped upstairs and slipped on my lucky, silky, black boxer shorts and draped myself on the settee. We enjoyed a glass of wine or two and fell asleep. How disappointing!

However, before we got up the next morning, the most incredible three events happened. Firstly, the previous evening's lost intimate moment was recaptured, which was amazing! Secondly, my wife got up and made me the most fantastic, full English breakfast with well-done toast. Thirdly, I woke up!

Cliff Slade
Tenbury Wells

Writing is a kind of a self-communication for me; it's that bit of sanctuary. As a child I lacked the confidence to practise skills to communicate with others, so I communicated with, and listened to, myself. Sometimes it made sense, and other times it didn't, but it really didn't matter because I always worked things out myself anyway! I didn't wait to let people tell me what to do or how to do it – I decided myself.

I felt comfortable with my inner communication, but unless I was destined to become a monk and take an oath of communication abstinence from the rest of the world, I had to, at some point, find my voice! Throughout infant and primary school, I managed to skip speaking to my teachers but eventually some effort was made between the school and my mum to encourage me to speak in class and interact with the lesson. Questions were being asked as to why I didn't speak. I was asked by my mum and the teacher why I didn't speak to the teacher in class. I didn't answer! The teacher said 'next time in class, I will ask you for an answer when all the other pupils put their hands up'. That moment came and the incredible pain I suffered was agonising! As planned, everyone put their hands up and the teacher said 'Clifford'. The whole world stopped. The whole class looked at me as if to say in unison 'what, Clifford! Clifford never says anything. This is going to be good!' I broke out in a hot sweat and clasped my hands tight together; my heart was beating so hard and loud the whole class could hear it; my mouth completely dried up and I went as red as a hot, freshly boiled beetroot. The silence was deafening but the muffled sniggers were ear piercing and time literally stopped! I didn't say anything! Eventually, my other classmates started losing interest at my silence, and so did the teacher, and the question was dished out elsewhere. For the rest of that lesson and the rest of my life, I was left mortified, embarrassed, shamed and in constant, unbearable fear of being laughed at or put on the spot, or asked to speak in a group or in public again! I thereafter became a master of adopting strategies to evade situations where I was expected to be involved, to speak, or to converse in any way.

Throughout the rest of my schooldays and thereafter in my social, personal, work, business and private life, I had to find a way to address this constant fear or I was going nowhere and achieving nothing as my life and character were evolving. Even today and every day, that fear I felt that day very much remains with me. It seemed everything I ever wanted to do was always on the other side of being afraid, and that trepidation and that dread had to be conquered! I didn't say to my inner self, 'I wish I could', I said 'I will' – and I did!

I really did need to find my voice and stand up and speak and to be heard!

For me, writing a speech and preparing a speech is exactly the same as writing a letter. It's a little story to an audience and it has to have a pace, rhythm and format. In a letter, you are physically anonymous, but the big difference in a speech is that you have to stand up and deliver it – in person. What, me? As I progressed through work, I made many speeches and presentations. I had to as I was a chargehand, then a supervisor, assistant manager, manager, commercial manager, director and managing director. Isn't that strange that an ordinary folk like me was transforming a stumbling block into a stepping stone?

This is a speech I wrote and delivered. This is the biggest speech of a father's life! The first address at my daughter's wedding on her big day. As I stood up then, and whenever I stand up to speak even today, without fail, I feel the same pain and fear that was so intolerable and excruciating in that classroom all those years ago!

Family and friends, it is a great pleasure to have you with us in our humble family home. On behalf of Julie, Paul and Carrie, we welcome you to Charlie and Beth's very special day.

Just by the fact that you are here today means you are the nearest and dearest to Charlie and Beth, so a big thank you for sharing this day with them, particularly those who have travelled so far – you really have made their day. Looking around, I feel Charlie and Beth really will appreciate the effort everyone has put into looking absolutely fantastic today.

It is very difficult to put into words what today means to me – to take my daughter's hand and walk her down the aisle one of the proudest and most emotional duties as a father I have ever performed or experienced. As well as a huge relief that she is finally off my payroll.

Beth looks absolutely beautiful and stunning today. As I gave her away today, I couldn't help reminiscing about that moment in time when she was brought into the

world in the maternity ward as we both re-
covered from the shock of becoming parents
for the first time. We had one of those
special, golden moments. We were both
holding our precious new arrival - our
eyes met, we both welled up and Julie said
those three little words that will stay
with me forever, 'it's a monkey'. So many
of you here today came into the hospital
and also agreed that Beth did actually
look like a baby monkey.

But of course, to her dad she was
nothing but the most edible, beautiful baby I could ever wish for. I must admit she
did act like a little monkey sometimes.
There was that one time when Beth asked
her Auntie Annie to come and play with her
in the Wendy house and then smacked poor
Auntie Annie over the head with a heavy-
based frying pan. You saw stars and have
never been quite right since…

Beth also demanded serious attention
at times: Julie was talking on the telephone to her sister one day. Beth wanted
to talk to her about something. So how did
Beth get her mother's attention? She simply found a pair of scissors and cut
through the telephone cable whilst her
mother was in mid-conversation leaving her
just holding the handset in shock!

I really felt for Chris, her cousin at
this time. He really was a victim of

Beth's. As soon as Beth set eyes on poor old Chris she would scream and terrorise him to the extent we really did have to keep Beth away from him. At the age of twenty-four, Chris is only now trusting the opposite sex.

Obviously, Charlie, I would not share all this with you until after you had actually exchanged vows.

Eventually, off Beth went to school and she soon developed into a clever, popular girl. Academically, Beth regularly made us feel total opposites – at times proud and at times perplexed. Proud: at the age of fifteen she gained grade eight on clarinet and grade five on piano, which is an incredible talent and level to attain. Perplexed: as she was studying and revising for her history GCSE, she said, closing her history book, 'so Winston Churchill was a German then'!

After school and college, Beth moved to Liverpool and spent three years at university. By now, she was becoming an independent, confident, mature AND A VERY EXPENSIVE young woman. As a student you expect hard times but Beth was the only student seen to be shopping in Marks and Spencer's. However, all that expensive brain food paid off as she graduated with a 2:1 honours degree in English literature which again we are immensely proud of.

Whilst she was living in Liverpool, strangely, she met someone. I say, strangely, because it wasn't someone from Liverpool, it was a local guy.

As a father, it is quite natural to quietly investigate who this new male friend is, and as a Freemason, unsuitable candidates can be quietly spirited away.

- I found out that his name was Charlie.
- I found out that he had won the title of the strongest man in Tenbury (that was a good quality – he could look after and protect Beth).
- I found out that he had his own town flat (that demonstrated he was able to manage his own finances and provide for Beth).
- I found out that he was a farmer (so he had a job and was obviously a hardworking, young man) and Beth, spookily, always said that she would marry a farmer.
- I found out that he was a very talented rugby player and all-round sportsman.
- I found out that he was public school educated (so he was obviously well placed and able to help Beth with her history knowledge and Winston Churchill).

I did eventually meet Charlie Fernihough, and it was clear it was serious,
and today Charlie really is the dashing
groom.

Julie and I are delighted that Beth
has chosen to marry Charlie. He is everything we would have wished for in a son-
in-law. He is a hard-working, caring, protective and supportive guy. Many of Charlie's friends are here today, and I know
they will agree what a loyal friend he is,
and at a moment's notice, he would come to
help anyone.

I really warmed to Charlie and had a
great deal of respect for him when on the
thirteenth of February 2011 (last year)
Charlie telephoned me and asked for my
blessing as he was going to propose to
Beth the next day on Valentine's Day. I
had a very excited Beth call me, not only
informing me Charlie had proposed, but he
had also presented an engagement ring.

The following twelve months were to be
a real roller coaster – wedding plans and
a date was almost immediately fixed (today). However, probably around three
months after the engagement, Charlie
started having second thoughts. He just
could not cope with Beth and she was proving to be so difficult that he really
could not see them being able to live together as she really was unbearable.

Beth herself thought she was seriously ill and going totally mad and wondering why she was behaving the way she was. Weeks went by and Beth decided to go to the doctors to address her mood swings and behaviour and – hey presto all was apparent. Her serious illness was – she was pregnant!

Strangely, I did not see or hear from Charlie for some time. But Charlie immediately wrapped his big arms around her and nurtured her just like one of his pregnant ewes, but in reality, it was more like one of his pregnant pigs.

We all know at Christmas, Scarlett was born, and they are both brilliant, natural, loving, proud parents – Scarlett thriving on the love and care she gets from them both. Scarlett could not wish for better parents, and there is only one person who came near to upstaging the bride today – Scarlett.

I just want to say, Beth became pregnant, had a baby and started two businesses (which are proving lucrative). Beth has totally organised every detail of this wedding today, which is an incredible achievement alongside being a new mum. Again, that could have only been achieved with Charlie's support.

I am coming to the end now: as father of the bride, it is tradition that I offer the first toast. That tradition is probably afforded to me because it is expected I am paying for this grand occasion. However, I am grateful and thank Charlie's parents, Paul and Carrie for completely sharing the costs of today.

Finally, Charlie, I want to say to you. Not only has Beth been a remarkable daughter, she is now proving to be a remarkable mother and I know she will be a remarkable wife. Both Julie and I, and all our family have a great deal of love and affection for Beth. It is that love and affection we now extend to you and welcome you to our family. I also know your family has also embraced Beth in the same way.

Every father hopes for a wonderful man to marry his daughter, and I don't believe they come any better than you, Charlie. Carrie and Paul have done a great job on you as a son, and I have no doubt you will make a great husband for Beth.

So, ladies and gentlemen, I would like to propose a toast to the new Mr & Mrs - Fernihough.

Ladies and gentlemen, whilst Charlie and Beth remain seated, would you please be upstanding for the toast. I give you Beth and Charlie. Breathe - thank god for that!

New Member of our Family – Welcome Charlie

There are many disadvantages of being brought up in a single-parent family, particularly in the sixties, as it was very rare. As a child, I just wanted to be the same as everyone else and didn't want to be noticed. When other kids talked about their dads playing football, going off somewhere, making something, learning something, watching them, helping them, teaching them, buying them things, reading with them, swimming with them, I just didn't have any of those experiences, so at an early age I had to invent multiple responses to questions like, 'why isn't your dad watching you play in the school football match?'

and 'why isn't your dad at the school parents' evening?' and so on. I felt different, I felt sad and I felt something was missing. It was akin to bereavement, although my dad was like a ghost and he did pop up to see me now and again!

Similarly, and perversely, there are advantages in growing up without a dad figure. Although I didn't know this at the time, one positive element was that I didn't have a father figure to advise me, show me or tell me, so this just further endorsed and expanded my already advanced ability to work things out myself and make my own decisions. As they were my own decisions and made by me and me alone, they were always right. As I was always right, my character developed with a positive outlook and I am the most positive individual I know or have ever come across. What we are visualising very much depends on what we are looking for and I was always looking at what was in front of me now and worked with that. I always felt good and I was always happy. I would be, wouldn't I? No past or future, just now to enjoy!

Likewise, without a father figure, for the same reasons, I didn't have anyone to criticise me. My mother hardly criticised me either because she was too busy being a one-parent family and providing for us. Without criticism, I had no fear of being wrong and no compass of disapproval or condemnation!

This positivity, coupled with my not having a critical upbringing, became my destiny, and nothing in this world will stop me from doing something if I want to do it. This is one of the reasons why I am able to stand up and speak, despite without fail, every single time, I experience the absolute agonising fear, panic and dread I go through just before I stand up to speak. This fear is the fear and experience that I felt that day in school when I was asked to speak. I feel the fear and do it anyway but still feel that awful pain! When I did what I feared, that fear wasn't there! I wasn't just going through life, I was growing through life and breathing and trusting and believing in myself. That's what I am and that's what I had. I couldn't go wrong. I could do anything!

These elements, with many others, are interwoven into much of my personal, work, social and life achievements.

As mentioned, speeches come in many forms: happy, sad, business and others; again, I feel they are just letters. This next one I wrote and delivered as an address at my dad's funeral - serious stuff!

```
            THE OLD MAN'S ADDRESS
To  some  people,  he  was  known  as  Ken  or
Kenny.  To  Pauline,  Glenn  and  me  he  was  al-
ways  known  as  'The  Old  Man'.  Even  when  he
was  young  he  was  The  Old  Man.
```

Life success and achievements are difficult to measure. I can't stand here and say The Old Man was well-travelled; he never ever had a passport, he wasn't a rocket scientist nor was he rich and famous. But of course, to his children and grandchildren, he was incredibly rich and successful. The Old Man lived a rich life through its simplicity. He was more than happy and extremely content in his own company, visiting his family, or going around town picking up his bits and pieces of daily shopping. He was fiercely independent and was certainly a creature of habit. If any of us visited him and, on the odd occasion he was not at home, you could almost certainly look at your watch and identify his whereabouts.

He loved a bet on the horses and he loved a go on the lottery and a few years ago he loved going fishing. It was not unusual to see eels swimming in the bath, and it was also not unusual to see them escaped from the bath and wriggling on the floor! Only weeks ago, Glenn would still take him jellied eels.

He absolutely loved his food. It wasn't a curry for him, a stir-fry or a pizza, but he loved a weekly Ambleside fish and chips. He was a fantastic cook and if you were lucky enough to have a meal cooked by The Old Man, you were certainly in for a treat. Without exception it was the best meat and the freshest vegetables, carefully prepared all morning, and cooked with love and care.

Although not financially rich, he was never short. He knew how to make a few bob by using his charm, cheek, charisma or humour – or in challenging situations all four at the same time. It was not unusual to be regularly presented with huge bags full of the best vegetables, best meat or fish and you can bet a deal had been done and a bargain got.

He was always smartly dressed, with shoes well-polished. He also had a wicked sense of humour and most of the time it was at someone else's expense. His face-pulling and dry humour and 'mickey taking' was with him right up to a few weeks ago. This simple, no frills service and funeral were requested and planned nineteen years ago, in every detail, by him. Not sure if he was having a laugh, but he stated he wanted his ashes scattering – he just didn't say where!

One absolute feature of his personality which never ever faltered, was his equality whether he was helping Pauline becoming a turkey tycoon, watching Glenn play football or fishing – he was proud of us all in equal measure. If ever he said directly to one of us 'you have done alright', it was always followed immediately with, 'well, you have all done well.'

This also extended without equivocation to his grandchildren, Beth, Carl, Michael and Katie. He absolutely loved them to bits and was so proud of them. Again, he never singled one of them out for praise. 'All four of them are beautiful kids and they have all done well,' he would say. And he also extended that love to Pauline's dogs and would often be found dog-sitting.

For many, many years, every Saturday morning, we would make the journey to Worcester from Tenbury and The Old Man, with his grandad hat on, would make Beth and Michael a full English breakfast. This was a much-looked-forward-to, weekly event which even today, is a great memory for them. I know Carl and Katie have similar fond memories. He was always generous towards them and he never missed a birthday card to them, and there was always a few bob inside.

Last year, The Old Man was indeed getting old and we celebrated his eightieth birthday with him all together. Carl baked him a cake, and a candle was lit and we all sang 'happy birthday'. He blew the candle out and said how great that was. Typically, he shrugged his shoulders and his words were 'I haven't achieved much' and then he reflected and said 'well, I'll tell you what I have achieved: I have been lucky enough to see all of you grow up. There are not many people who can say that.'

More recently, he became a great-grandad, and we took Scarlett to visit him and despite his fragility and confused state, he almost turned back the clock twenty years with a flick of a switch and said she was beautiful. He held her, kissed her and said 'welcome to the family.'

Finally, as a friend or relative, The Old Man' would always help anyone, in whatever way he could. He was never needy or wanted any attention. He never complained and never asked for anything. He was always grateful for his health even when he was obviously ill or uncomfortable, and most importantly, he was always so grateful and thankful to Glenn, Angie, Carl and Katie for bearing the brunt of caring for him over the past few years.

To us all he was a character and he will be missed.

As well as my own painful and challenging inhibitions about just standing up and speaking, nothing prepared me for how difficult that was to deliver; I only just made it to the end! Nothing prepared me for the moment I looked up and viewed all my close family upset and in tears. Nothing prepared me for the emotion of my son, Michael, carrying his grandad in and out of the chapel and how upset he was. Nothing prepared me for the absolutely fantastic poem my daughter Beth read out without a single falter. Nothing prepared me for my nephew and niece, Carl and Katie's excellently-worded and -executed memory of their grandad! Nothing prepared me for my own emotion.

The Old Man couldn't swim but he loved fishing and being near the canal or river. After some time following the funeral and cremation, we collected The Old Man's ashes from the undertaker. Having no instruction as to what to do with his ashes, collectively we all agreed and decided to scatter his remains across Worcester race course 'Pitchcroft'. He loved Pitchcroft. He worked there regularly. He loved horse racing. Pitchcroft was next to the river where he fished and, from time to time, when we were young children, he took us there for walks near the boating quay. So, on a wet, dull, blustery day, everyone took turns scattering his ashes across Pitchcroft and in particular, around a tree, which in itself looked like we were some sort of bizarre cult exercising a ritual! For this reason, I declined to take my turn. As well as it being very windy, it seemed everyone was getting a mouthful of The Old Man's ashes, much to everyone's amusement. We also found it very funny how much of his ashes there were.

Everyone seemed to be having about four goes chucking him across the race course until the transparent, plastic urn, that resembled a sweet jar, was empty. Nothing prepared us for the hilarity the next day when we learnt that the River Severn had burst its banks, completely flooding Pitchcroft, and we all laughed as we estimated that the old man was now downstream in and around the Bristol Channel area!

Father, mother, son and daughter relationships are complicated, but it seems a daughter's character and behaviour can be greatly affected by her father's relationship with her and similarly a son's relationship with his mother can have the same impact. Collectively, and to quote that well-known phrase – 'it's your parents who fuck you up'!

This next letter I would like to write now just to hear what comes out! My dad passed away April 2012, so that was many years ago!

Wednesday, 09 August, 2017

Dear Dad,

This is the first time I've ever addressed you as Dad. You have never heard me call out your name as 'Dad', have you? It's a difficult word for me to say because I never had the opportunity to practise using it! I really missed you as a figure in my life and it was quite difficult without you. I missed you at my first day at school. I was just dropped off at

the school gate and walked in on my own. I
clung to the wall outside the classroom
and couldn't stop crying. I always walk on
my own now, but I've never cried since! I
missed you at my first and only birthday
party; it was really good – jelly and
evaporated milk and all that. We even had
that new stuff, Dream Topping, on our tri-
fle with hundreds and thousands. I went
bright red when everybody sang 'happy
birthday!' You should have seen me playing
my first game of football for the school.
Actually, you didn't miss much. I was goal
keeper and let a few in. I've never been
sports-minded really as no one ever
watched me. You missed loads of things but
it doesn't matter. Did you miss me?

Our mum always said that you said that
I wasn't yours. I know that is not true
because we are so alike. I can see so much
of you in me. Did you even say that and if
you did, why did you say it? We do say
some terrible and unpleasant things when
people row, but it did hurt to be told
that! It's as if you didn't want me or
want to know me. That wasn't true was it?
Our mum also said that you were always
drunk and hit her and never gave her a
penny towards bringing me up! I know there
are always two sides to a story and I've
only ever heard our mum's side, so who
knows why or if you were like this? I nev-

er ever saw you drunk or aggressive. Were you?

Were you shy and self-conscious as a boy? I am so self-conscious it hurts but I'm dealing with it. I'm quite good now at not going red and doing things in life!

I went into two children's homes when I was five and eight. It was awful. I even had to go to a different school! Why didn't I come to live with you? Why didn't you come and get me? Mum had a couple of breakdowns. She couldn't cope. It wasn't nice. She was always crying. Where were you? Why didn't you come?

Thanks for the birthday and Christmas cards – the money was always great. I even bought some savings stamps at school! Every now and then you took me out to Barbourne Park and I had a whole bottle of Corona pop and a Mr Whippy ice cream with a flake. I really liked going to the pub as well as having a ride in your car.

Thanks for coming to my wedding. I think that was the first time you came to a significant happening in my life. I'm sure there were reasons that you couldn't come to the other things, but it was great to have you at the church, but a shame you couldn't come to the after-do. It was really good and I had to stand up and thank everyone for coming. I started off with 'my wife and I', and everyone laughed!

Thank you for being such a fantastic grandad to Beth and Mike. They really loved you, and I could see you really loved them. You always hugged them and gave them loads of kisses! Why didn't you kiss or hug me? You never did once! I find it really difficult and I rarely hug or kiss family or friends because it feels really awkward and uncomfortable. Is that what it was like for you? I try to avoid it at all times. Nasty old things those touchy-feely moments, but did you love me as much as you loved Beth and Mike? That's when I really saw you being a dad – when you were a grandad.

Sorry that I didn't stay with you in hospital at the end. It wasn't because I didn't love you; it was because I didn't know how to love you! I wanted to hold you in your hospital bed in those last moments but I didn't know how to hold you! I didn't want to wake you up and stop to talk to you at the end because I didn't know what to say! I didn't stay to the end because I didn't want to cry, because I don't know how to cry! You looked so peaceful and never looked so good when I left you, but I think you had already gone!

I wrote and stood up and did an address at your funeral. Did you like it? It wasn't easy.

Thank you for being a great grandad,
thank you for creating my personality and
thank you for being my dad.
Sorry I allowed my name to change from
Sampson to Slade, and I hope you enjoyed
your trip down the River Severn!

Cliff

Certain pictures remind me of a moment and feeling in time. One of those pictures follows shortly. The moment I first went to school I realised through my classmates' interactions that I was different to everyone else, inasmuch as I did not have a father living at home as everyone else did.

For over a week, the Worcester News were publishing pictures of first-year starters at various schools, so I wrote a letter and it was published with the accompanying picture.

The picture was just of my brother, my sister and me. My mother had taken the picture on one of the first Kodak cameras with a square four-flash bulb unit mounted on top of the camera. I distinctly remember crossing my fingers for the flash bulb to work as it was my mum's third or fourth attempt at taking the picture, and she was getting cross as the camera kept failing to work. My fingers were crossed and that momentary feeling of trepidation and anxiety were recorded in that snap forever!

Dear Editor,

For some new school starters into our education system, they are completing their first term and half term is upon them. In the Worcester News, we are now seeing children's first term immaculate class photographs appearing. I recall my first day at Warndon Primary School in 1965 (photo attached). There was no pre-school induction or nursery class. It was into our shorts, blazers and caps, and for my sister, Pauline, a beret, with ties (not elasticated) and polished shoes (with animal foot prints and compass built into the soles). We were dropped off (after walking two miles) outside the school gate and pointed in the direction of the school door. Phew! How daunting was that! At least I had my brother, Glenn and sister to walk to school with, albeit they were a few classes up in the primary school!

I think that Warndon Primary School is now called an academy, and sweatshirts and long trousers are now the drill. How casual!

At this time, we still had to wait almost a decade before we even entered Europe!

Cliff Slade
Tenbury Wells

Didn't look as if I wanted to talk much, did I? (I'm the little one – with fingers crossed!)

Whenever anyone makes a comment about letters that I have written, they always mention the humour: 'it made me chuckle', 'it made me laugh', 'your letters are so funny', and suchlike. Where does the humour come from?

The ridiculous letter that follows was penned because in previous news issues, the likes of dog fouling, traffic problems, immigration, Donald Trump and his executive orders, a new bridge and a potential new Tesco were all topics, so I encapsulated the lot.

Dear Sir,

Through your column, would you allow me to announce my intention to stand as a candidate in the forthcoming May 2017 Worcestershire County Council elections?

I have some business experience but no political knowledge or understanding. I pledge, on the behalf of the people of Tenbury, to build a wall between Tenbury and Burford. This will ease the traffic flow into Tenbury which has blighted the town for all too long! Tenbury will not accept any new outside settlers originating from Ludlow, Leominster, Burford or St. Michaels forthwith!

I will immediately sign an executive order to scrap the replacement bridge at Eastham and replace it with a manual boat ferry crossing (40p per crossing).

The new Tesco store will not be allowed to open as a supermarket and the site and building will become the new home for Tenbury Museum.

In order to address the dog fouling issue in our town, Tenbury will become a complete 'no dog town'. On my inauguration, all dogs will be removed via the new Tenbury Transport Trust vehicle, and the

drivers will become dog catchers and war-
dens! However, as I am Uncle Cliff to two
lovely whippets called Whizz and Flash,
they will be the only canines allowed in
Tenbury!
Worse things have happened!

Cliff Slade
County Council Candidate
Tenbury Wells

Humour is another strategy I mastered to get me out of, and get me into situations. Humour is a great tool to deflect an answer that I couldn't answer, to deflect from my incredible self-consciousness and the horrible bright red face I exhibited when I was put in the spotlight or was looked at or spoken to. One mini-moment of humouring deflected that spotlight away from me and gave me the opportunity to recover or prepare myself. I still use this tool even today!

One of the most embarrassing memories of being so painfully self-conscious and totally embarrassed, again, within school, was having to don a bloody Christmas hat, not only in the classroom, which was excruciating enough, but then parade around the school hall. This was prior to my strategy time so I just suffered the torture. My hat was a great tall wizard-looking hat with crepe paper and a Chinese lantern hanging from it, I think to assimilate a Crimbo tree. God knows who made it or where it came from? Unbeknown to me, and just to make matters worse, on entering the hall the bloody thing was too tall to go under the door and it landed on the floor behind me detaching the lantern! This coupled with the big, red torch below the hat (my bloody red face) resulted in me making a right fool of myself.

I developed my humour to shock; it was the sort of humour you were thinking but it was too outspoken to express verbally. Whatever I was thinking that was funny, I just had to say it, irrespective of the consequences which made it even funnier for me! I can honestly say that I have never upset anyone or failed to raise a giggle with this tactic, which demonstrates how effectively, efficiently and subtly I had mastered this particular style. It was the sort of approach which left the person or group I was interacting with thinking, 'did he really say that?' Of course, this style was an aggressive line of attack that quickly repelled and redirected the focus and attention away from me!

An example of this involved my local news agent shop and its proprietor, a guy called 'Don'. When I buy a newspaper in the morning, I always have a good laugh and joke with him, one to one, which is fine. Don is extrovert, out-going and naturally amusing. At the time, he was naturally concerned and worried as to the impact a new Tesco store, that had just opened, would have on his business. The whole town was split on whether this new store was a welcome or unwelcome addition. One morning it was very busy in the shop, there was a long queue and I'm standing at the back of the line with people starting to join me from the rear. Don had spotted me and was about to say something to me which would obviously have put me in an exposed position (under the spot light!) My defensive strategy dynamically kicked in and an attack statement was quickly needed and fired. I said 'come on Don, pull your finger out. You don't have to queue and wait like this in Tesco.' This immediately reduced everyone to laughter and left poor old Don speechless and everyone making and adding their own comments – phew! Another disaster averted!

This method is also in my writing and subtle, crafty lines or paragraphs, at times leave the reader thinking 'did he really write that?' as well as raising a smile!

Try saying what you are thinking when your moral mind or natural instinct is telling you to zip it. It really is empowering, enlightening, liberating and amusing as long as you don't get a black eye. This technique does need a great deal of practising and judgement - good luck!

Many times, I have written a letter and sent it to the media in someone else's name. Yes, of course, with their permission. I do this just to liven things up and change direction with a bit of narcissism thrown in! I love Oscar Wilde and his quotes and quips, especially this one: 'there is only one thing in the world worse than being talked about, and that is not being talked about'.

This is one of my letters contradicting my previous printed letter with tongue-in-cheek using my mate's name and ID. People did stop me, having actually believed it, and say 'hey, that guy didn't think much of your proposals', which made it even funnier for me knowing I had written the letter myself. I think that I invented fake news!

Dear Mr Editor,
    Cliff Slade's letter is long on rhetoric and short on logic. As a tax payer, I would like to know how Mr Slade proposes to pay for a structure separating Tenbury from Burford. Also, although the new Tesco store's arrival in the town has in the past divided the town, I think his change of use of the store into a museum is totally barmy!
    As Slade commences his campaign, he will quickly realise Tenbury Transport is managed and depends on volunteers and transferring them into dog catchers is highly unlikely! I, for one, will look forward to his ill-thought out manifesto which includes a blanket dog owning ban in the town quickly coming back to bite him in the bum!
    Similarly, his proposed scrapping of Eastham Bridge, and replacing it with a 40p crossing fee, is far too cheap and is destined for financial failure and we, as

tax payers, will have to pick up the pieces.
I hope the electorate of Worcestershire are not seduced by his Trump style
antics!

Mr A N Other
(AKA Cliff Slade)

I even wrote a letter debasing myself and signed it
off myself and it was published. No one said anything to
me, other than a couple of people asking for clarification,
'did I write that letter?', 'hmmmm, yes, I did!'

Dear Editor,
Over the past two months we have had
to endure a weekly letter from Cliff
Slade! Could I please make a plea to the
editor and the 'Opinion' page to give us a
break from his egotistical, pointless musings and appeal to Mr Slade to find an al-
ternative outlet for his beliefs, judgements and reflections of our town, its
people and commerce! He is not funny; he
is not clever and completely spoils negativity, pessimism, cynicism and detracts
from more important issues such as Brexit,
Tesco and hedgehog safety!

Cliff Slade
Tenbury Wells

Success, whenever it is experienced, and even when it is just a letter being published and liked, feels good and gives you confidence. I really do believe I am successful in everything I do; I never wait for something to happen as it would never happen. This philosophy evolved on the back of my humour attack strategy, but life is serious sometimes and you can't just jump and treat life as if you're a clown jumping into a circus ring all the time. For example, if I am entering a room, meeting or gathering with business colleagues, family, friends or others, I will again use my attack strategy, but minus the humour and will attack by being the first to talk, interact, smile, nod and engage which puts the rest of the people, collectively or individually, on a back foot that takes the dreaded spotlight away from me and on to them!

One sticky moment, not a mistake but an experience I learnt from and never allowed it to happen again, involved Julie, who was taking her first steps into her English teaching career and teaching at a private school. Schools have teachers and teachers are within a layer of my subconscious as a 'no go' area, and at this particular time in my life, I was still a little reluctant to converse with this type of individual in our society. Eek teachers! Here I was in the school hall and it was parents' evening, followed by a parents' stuffy charity raising event. To cut a long story short, teachers, parents and the bloody headteacher were talking to me, and Julie took it on her own back to jump in and answer on my behalf (which is another story!) and I stood there like some gormless idiot catching flies! It was like 'Crackerjack' when Lesley Crowther kept jumping in over Peter Glaze. It was almost as funny as it was embarrassing. I didn't need that, and it never happened again because whenever I entered a room after that or found myself in those situations, I was armed and prepared with my 'humour' or 'speak first' attack strategy. I never make the same mistake twice and this was another momentous, evolutionary moment of my developing character armoury. It was my voice and I wanted it to be heard and exercised by me. At this time, when I walked into a room, I was conscious of the people in the room liking me. I now walk into a room thinking, do I like them?

At times and at random, I write a short letter of observation, experience or just something that has amused my simple mind!

Dear Letters,
        Tenbury Community Care.
        As I am getting older, I really appreciate living in Tenbury even more. Not only is it a lovely place with nice people, we really do get a sense of being part of a community with so much going on. Further to this, personally, I have just received an invitation from my Doctor's surgery in-

viting me to an annual health review. How
thoughtful is that! This morning I received a further letter from my surgery
informing me 'given my age category' I was
entitled to and welcome to receive a flu
vaccination. Crikey, I hope 'Caldicott's'
are not having any January sales!

Cliff Slade
Tenbury Wells

'Caldicott's' are our local undertaker. This is another
in the same category as the one before.

ADRIAN'S 'FOCUS' FURORE!
Whether one agrees, disagrees or is impartial to Adrian Kibbler's recent 'Focus'
article on education results and Brexit, I
really do sense a little mischievousness
from the wiry, old journalist! I do generally find his 'Focus' features thought-
provoking, interesting, impartial and maybe, at times, perhaps a little of his personal view. However, on this occasion, he
really did press a few buttons, with a
passionate response from Brian Griffiths
and Ron Hill, respectively (Advertiser
29/09/2016). Their respective letters made
good reading with differing views and reflections as well as educating us on past
associated key moments in time! With the
Advertiser's letters column flagging of

late, Adrian Kibbler's Focus piece probably achieved its intended purpose and he
is almost certainly chuckling in his cra-
vat! I must say, in contrast to Brian
Griffith's view, I like our small local
paper with its 'hatched, matched and despatched columns! In my view, differing political views are also healthy. Further to
this, historical education results, levels
and standards will always be debated. For
better or worse we will one day say 'remember when we were in Europe' and 'bring
back grammar schools' - I hope they
doesn't!

Cliff Slade
Tenbury Wells

In my letter to the 'old man', I alluded to a couple of
occasions that I had had the pleasure of spending some
time in a couple of children's homes in my early years on
two separate occasions. I didn't know at the time but I do
know now that I was sent to these homes with my brother
and sister to give my mum some respite and recovery time
from, not only bringing us up on her own, but also to deal
with the shock and despair of a new introduction to our
family unit of a new sister for me, Judith, who was born
with a life expectancy of nil, with a new condition called
'spina bifida.' Judith was born paralysed from the waist
down and in need of an immediate emergency operation

to save her life! So, at an early age, I was packed off to a children's home!

Where was the old man? Where were my uncles and aunts? Where were my godparents: Aunty Pat, Uncle Michael and Aunty Beryl? They were my family! They were my family and godparents for moments like this, weren't they? I have never been close to my uncles or aunties, never really had a relationship with them. After this, why would I?

I never met my grandparents. Both sets of my grandparents were all long gone (as in, passed away), so I didn't have any grandparents to scoop me up or even grow up with, which was very sad because grandparents can bring so much to a child and his and her developments and, at times, I'm sure, fill in the emotional gaps.

My mum was having a breakdown and medical issues because of the arrival and condition of my new sibling, who we had been preparing for as a new addition to our family over the last nine months. She was not only severely disabled but she was almost certainly going to die. I didn't know what disabled was, other than someone told me that Judith would not be able to walk – if she survived! So, let's quickly just take stock. I'm seven years old. I've got no dad. My mum is understandably having mental and medical health issues. My new sister is severely disabled and about to die and I'm removed from my home to be put with some strange people I've never met before! All

I wanted to be was the same as everybody else. No wonder I didn't speak to anyone for the next ten years. I was probably in bloody shock as well as dealing with the greatest challenge in my short life so far – going to bloody school!

In this first care home, I can remember walking around thinking, what's happening? Is my mum OK? I didn't understand someone dying so I wasn't too concerned about that, albeit it wasn't a nice feeling. Would I go home again? I just wanted to play with my toys at home. I wanted to go home! I was also being told about and prepared for going to school for the first time in my life. I didn't know what was going to happen. I was insecure, and my stomach felt as if it was turning over. It wasn't nice. I felt upset, confused and sad.

Besides this whole experience, I encountered a significant incident within this placement, which itself was insignificant but had a profound impact on my life, personality, temperament, behaviour and character, from that moment to this.

On the very first day at this home, whilst playing outside with my brother, sister and other children, I can remember being pushed, and brushed up against the wall. It was all good fun; we were having so much fun and I forgot where I was! I can remember a white wire or sort of cable running down the wall; it was fastened to the wall by little clips. I brushed up against this cable while we were playing and slightly pulled it away from the wall, dislodging a cable clip so it slightly hung loose.

We were all called inside for something to eat. I was starving and couldn't wait to eat. We all eagerly went and sat around the table. We were ready to be served with food when a lady, presumably the lady whose house it was, came in so cross and angry, shouting and demanding to know who had broken and ripped the wire off the wall. It was the telephone wire to the house! She was so mad. My brother, Glenn, immediately pointed at me and said 'it was him!' I was mortified, and this lady took me outside and showed me the cable. It was broken, snapped, severed. I didn't do that! I only accidentally dislodged it from the wall. It wasn't me – someone else must have got caught up in it after me, disturbing the wire! 'Did you do this?', she screeched. I had never been told off before. I had never been shouted at before. I was unable to tell her how it had become cut off. I couldn't work it out; all I knew was that it was, genuinely and honestly, not me. I was speechless and shook my head which just further provoked this already furious lady. I was unceremoniously marched to bed straight away. As I passed the dining room, everyone including my brother and sister were tucking into food and didn't even notice me, glance at me or were even bothered. I was being dragged off to bed for punishment for a crime I didn't commit! I was made to get into bed whilst the sun was shining. I was hungry, petrified and alone! The curtains were drawn, and I was told I was not allowed to come down until I had told the truth! I cried and cried and cried and cried – it wasn't me. I didn't do it! I wanted to go home! Where was my mum? Why wasn't I at home? I was vulnerable, I was alone, I was upset, I cried again and again. No one came to console me, put their hands around me or hold me when I needed to be held and comforted. Why couldn't I go home away from this strange place and strange people?

The sun set, and the summer evening turned to dusk, and I still cried on my own. The other children, including my brother and sister, came to bed. They told me what they had for dinner. I was so hungry. The lady came to me and asked me if I was ready to tell her I had broken this cable. I said, 'I didn't do it'. She asked me if I wanted something to eat and I said 'no!' I fell asleep; a sleep immersed in the fact that a wrong had taken place!

Next morning, I and everyone else, went down for breakfast. It was cornflakes. The lady said I had been chosen this morning to have the special dish. This special dish when I had eaten all my cornflakes would reveal a special treat. I spooned the dredges of the milk up and revealed the surprise at the bottom of the dish; it was a depiction of the cow jumping over the moon! Nothing was ever said about the severed wire, but it was etched on my character, forever! I think this lady awarded me this special attention to cheer me up, make me happier and bring me back into the social circle.

I was never counselled or had anything explained by anyone (not about the wire incident but the whole experience of the children's homes) – I just worked things out myself about what was going on in and around me. This moment was 'ground zero' and I could only pick myself up in a positive way or feel sorry and resentful for the rest of my life. There are many popular motivational quotes and the one that is the most meaningful to me is 'it's not how we fall. It's how we get back up again' by Patrick Ness.

I am so thankful for this moment. It was profound, as this was the birth of the incredible gift I was to develop to make my own decisions, be independent, observe, listen and conclude on my own! I knew being truthful to myself enabled me to be truthful and honest with others. I now knew justice, truth, integrity and being able to be heard through a life-changing moment of injustice was another key component of my developing persona. I knew everything without being told anything. I had grown up inside and I was on my own. I knew from that moment that I was on my own, and knowing that, gave me my future strength and determination.

Throughout my letters, and engrained in my character, is honesty, integrity and justice! If ever I feel that I or my family have a finger pointed at them unfairly, incorrectly or unduly, I will roar like a lion through the pen. One poor lady found this out when she absolutely unjustly accused my son of misbehaving, to the extent that she suggested she had been verbally and physically injured by his alleged actions! Her scathing letter was posted through my letter box. Her letter was full of inaccuracies; it was completely wrong and, more importantly, her accusations were incorrectly directed at my son! Within hours, my response below was hand posted through her letter box. I removed her identity for privacy.

Dear Mrs A.N. Other,

I am very sorry to hear you were involved in an accident outside the Regal Cinema on Monday the twenty fifth of September 2006. I am also concerned as a result of this accident you required hospital attention. I do hope your injuries do not have a lasting effect and you recover fully.

I hope I am a responsible individual, and as your letter is addressed to my wife, I am sure she would also consider herself responsible too.

I have no idea who you are, but if I may introduce one element of myself which I hope will support my respectability and responsibility. I have been a magistrate for some five years, currently serving in the West Mercia area. My wife, for her part, to support her responsibility, is a secondary school English teacher.

I hope I have brought my two children up to be honest, helpful, caring, considerate, courteous etc. – all attributes I feel my two children have in abundance. We, as parents, are also realistic, and not naive enough, to expect in the real world that we may encounter some minor misdemeanours as they grow up! To date, they have both grown into exemplary members of the community.

However, your letter is very ambiguous and full of inaccuracies. I, my wife, and more importantly, my son, consider these spurious insults and accusations in your letter most insulting and personal.

Firstly, this was not some group of lads but also females. They, like you, were leaving the cinema on conclusion of watching the film showing that evening.

You were knocked to the ground as a result of one female startling one male. This male was startled to the extent that it caused him to jump back and unbeknown to him, you were at the rear of him and a collision between you and him unfortunately occurred. This, in any one's interpretation, was an accident!

Michael, my son and Mr A.N. Other, whom you also named, were not in any way party to this incident. Apparently, the individual who collided with you, immediately apologised and offered assistance, and was genuinely sorry. I have also spoken to this individual, who takes full responsibility and also confirms that my son and Mr A.N. Other, or even any other person, played no part in this incident.

Yes, they were enjoying themselves and interacting in a humorous and fun way. THEY ARE EIGHTEEN YEARS OLD! Your accusation that they were all, as in a 'group of lads,' (including my son) pushing each other and larking around in a stupid manner without the respect or care of others around them, is a total untruth.

Your accusation that my son, or indeed any, of these individuals were *again* outside the cinema 'in the bus shelter larking about,' is again totally fabricated and untrue! My son was not even in Tenbury on the evening of the thirtieth of September, as he was attending a birthday party outside of Tenbury. It may be prudent to notify the individual/s who informed you of this to 'get their facts right'. It may also be sensible for you to check and double check your source/s before putting pen to paper.

My son has a car and a girlfriend, and he and I can assure you that he has better things to do and places to go than sitting in Tenbury bus shelter.

A.S.B.O. or 'Anti-social behaviour order' is obviously a term you are not familiar with. An A.S.B.O., as you refer to it, is directed by a court for *persistent* anti-social behaviour. In my experience an isolated ACCIDENT! does not and would not attract or even be associated with such an order!

I am copying your letter and my response to Mr and Mrs A.N. Other at Some Address. Mr A.N. Other (snr) is in fact a Police Officer and Mrs A.N. Other is also a teacher. I hope they will correct your correspondence too! I know Mr A.N. Other (jnr) and I could not speak of him more highly within a responsible, respectable context.

Through conversations with my son, I am also aware of the individual with whom you collided, and again, he is the total opposite of what you are recklessly branding these individuals as!

I find your last paragraph confrontational and threatening, and I will indeed be making your identity known to me with regard to taking this matter further to the correct authority or media to vindicate your false accusations. Further to this, your letter is also unfounded and untrue towards the other individual you have identified in your letter.

I do empathise with you that, not only have you been physically injured, but probably also mentally, but you must get your facts right and not be allowed to falsely accuse and generalise about individuals, in particular on this occasion, my son.

I would welcome and invite an immediate and unreserved written apology to my son in an effort to draw a line under your false finger pointing, and in order that I do not take this matter any further.

Mr Cliff Slade
Tenbury Wells

The poor lady was knocking on my door shaking and couldn't stop apologising the very next morning! Many years later she still tentatively side steps me in the street. I could write a separate book on writing letters of justice or injustice.

Looking back on my childhood, I genuinely feel I had a great childhood and I wouldn't change a thing. My wife, Julie, once said to me how could I say that and not be affected when my dad wasn't in my life, I went through two children's homes, my mum had breakdowns, I had a disabled sister, no grandparents and we had no money? I can only say that I had everything. Christmas was absolutely fantastic; I have so many great and special memories of Christmas. I had lots of great presents in a very big pillow case sack, sometimes two, which were all individually wrapped. And at the bottom of the sack was an orange and apple with monkey nuts. That's when I knew I had got to the bottom of the sack full of presents! Our house was always beautifully and festively decorated, as was our Christmas tree, which all added to the excitement. Christmas dinner was a huge cockerel from the milkman stuffed with stuffing and with all the accompaniments – we even had a new concept: Yeoman tinned new potatoes! Christmas pudding with cream was also beautiful; we only had cream at Christmas. As if that couldn't get better, we then had Christmas tea, which was equally eagerly awaited and amazing, with tinned salmon sandwiches, a Cadbury chocolate cake, jelly with a tin of evaporated milk and blancmange in those special glass moulds with tinned cherries on top! What about a tin of peaches and a tin of fruit cocktail with a tin of thick cream we had to shake until it thickened up? Throughout the day, I would then play with my Corgi toys, space hopper or ray gun, and look through my kaleidoscope. It really was fantastic, and no year was any different. I genuinely saw Father Christmas in his sleigh flying with Rudolf and the reindeers in the sky through my window on Christmas Eve – they really were special times! My mum really made this happen and paid for our presents and the food for the rest of the year via a Provident loan collector every week. What an effort! What a hero! What a memory! I carried over this Christmas spirit to my children, Beth and Mike, and I hope that spirit now lives in them. I really do love Christmas, albeit, our food is more refined these days, but the spirit is as strong as ever and lives on.

If ever I was ill, the doctor would be called, or I would be taken to the doctors' surgery. I was always cared for, kept warm, given special 'get well food' like bread and warm milk in a dish with sugar sprinkled over – how strange – but it worked. If ever I had a sore throat, I would be given dry toast – how bizarre! This is probably why, subsequently, I fashionably had my tonsils removed in hospital at the age of around nine. I always had an injection of penicillin into the cheek of my arse and how bloody painful was that, and my mum always held me down to enable this torture to be induced!

Birthdays were also so special because I always had lots of presents and I always felt special. I would also have many cards and money like a ten bob note and even a pound note sometimes. I would then walk around the corner to buy some sweets such as a Milk Tray bar, white chocolate mice, Aztec bar, Kali, coconut tobacco, chocolate toffee logs, American hard gums or Gold Nuggets chewing gum in a pull-string sack from the sweet shop, which is, incredibly, still there today! I had one birthday party in my life and it was a shared party between my brother and me. It was in our front room. We didn't have enough chairs to sit everyone on, so our mum put planks in between chairs with bed pillows on top of the plank, which trebled the seating capacity between two chairs! We played pass the parcel and I blew the candles out on my cake as everyone sang 'Happy Birthday'. How embarrassing, especially as someone slipped in the proverbial 'squashed tomatoes and stew'. Again, this was only my mum making this happen and paying for it. How did she do it on her own? My brother and sister all had the same, all the time!

Outside of special occasions, I was always well turned out and my shoes were always polished. I had plenty of new clothes like a parka long coat with the furry lined hood or home knitted gloves, jumpers and bobble hats! I always had new football boots and a football kit for school. I always had new school uniform and a home knitted school jumper. Again, my mum would then carefully budget to pay back all these costs to the weekly Provident loan collector!

I was always well fed and our food was amazing. Every Sunday, with the exception of one, we always had a roast dinner together as a family. The meat, particularly the beef and Yorkshire pud, were amazing. Later in the week, the dripping from the beef was then a healthy, hearty addition plastered onto 'Mother's Pride,' medium sliced bread! The one occasion we didn't have a roast was because half way through my mum cooking the roast, the gas meter ran out and needed some money, but on this occasion, we really didn't have any, so painfully, our half-cooked roast went uneaten and it was bread and jam that day! My mum's food, particularly egg and chips, was always the best. I was clean, warm and looked after. As I said I had a great childhood!

There are lots of facets to my emotions with our mum, which over time change by how she behaves and how I accept or reject her behaviour, views, opinions, beliefs, attitudes, values and respect. It is said the bond between a mother and son is sacred, special and remains unchanged by time or distance and this was true of this time. However, something was missing, and something was to develop!

At this time between the age of five and ten, probably the most formative period for a child when I was at home within the family unit, I had a great childhood. If I were to write a letter to my mum at this time it would be an honest, straightforward, simple correspondence.

Dear Mum,
    Thank you for some great Christmas and birthday times I had. I always had lots of presents and every last one was very special - the marbles, toy soldiers, Corgi cars and Action Men to name but a few. I always had everything and felt really grateful. Thanks for all the fantastic food I had; those roast dinners were amaz-

ing every Sunday. Homemade egg, chips and beans; bacon sandwiches; jam sandwiches; Shepherd's pie and peas; and the occasional Cadbury's smash!

Thanks for all the clothes, both hand-knitted and bought new, albeit, the hand-knitted ones in my last year at school at the age of sixteen were a bit embarrassing! It was very special as a child to go into town and choose a coat or be measured for a pair of shoes; thanks for allowing me to have those shoes with the animal foot prints on the sole and the compass in the inner sole. Everybody at school had them! Also, thank you for my new football boots and my complete green goalkeeper kit, which felt so good. I really did look and feel like Peter Bonetti, and at school with my kit and boots, I felt the same as everybody else, which was important!

Having a warm house with the coal fire roaring and the heat in the chimney toasting my toes in bed next to the chimney breast and those crisp, clean, folded cotton sheets with thick woollen blankets that kept me so warm, even when the inside bedroom window was iced over, were so very special and I was so thankful.

Thank you for those hot baths, clean clothes, clean football kit and polished shoes and boots. Thanks for the electric and gas meters you somehow kept topped up.

Wasn't it great when you had some money from the electric and gas meters rebated? Thanks for looking after me, buying me sweets, doughnuts at the bus stop in town, and for that birthday party, and what about that knickerbocker glory you bought me down the town – just me and you on my birthday! What about our song 'My Boy Lollipop'? Can you remember me singing 'Edelweiss' on your lap for three pence?

Experiencing how brave you were through those financial and emotional struggles in my early life with a young family, on your own as a single parent, has given me a great respect for the force, tenacity and reverence of not only you, but also for women in general.

Why did you hoodwink me into believing Father Christmas, the Easter bunny and the Tooth Fairy were real? How could you feed me with dry toast when I had a sore throat? How could you hold me down in an arm lock to enable the doctor to inject me with penicillin into the cheek of my arse? Why did you make me wear that plastic fold up rain hat to school? I know it was all for my good. Thanks for looking after me in the best possible way!

Thanks for a great childhood.

Cliff

Mixed into this time was my mum meeting someone else, Richard Slade, and getting married. He was OK with me but, to be honest, most of the time, he was out working. I have a few memories of him telling me off but 'Hey Ho', that was par for the course. Looking back, he took on the welfare and financial commitment of three children in the 1960s. He wasn't the sharpest tool in the box, and interacted with me very little, and I didn't gain any significant character, practical or academic developments from him, although he was a hard worker.

A consequence of this matrimony, my mum had a further child, a new half-sister for me, Judith. As mentioned earlier, Judith's disability and the understandable pressure of this time on my mum just to get Judith past her life expectancy of nil had an effect on the whole family, in particular on me, my home and my childhood security. So I spent some time in the children's homes, experiencing some life-changing and character-changing events.

Nothing can change the fantastic way I felt about my childhood, but later in life I would recognise that something in my developing personality and nature was missing. This missing link gave me an incredible, but arguable strength in business and management, but a difficult and challenging time lay ahead in my personal relationships with others, particularly in recognising that others loved me and needed to be loved back.

Although I was fed, watered, clothed and kept warm, I was never ever told I was loved. No one ever told me I was loved! My mum wasn't tactile, and I was never hugged, held or embraced. I never experienced intimacy. Our mum never sat and played with me. She didn't show me how to do a puzzle or read to me. I was never shown how to do practical things. Nearly sixty years on, I don't blame my mum, and I'm not going to even think about analysing, seeking the reason, vindicating her, rationalising or making allowances for my mum's behaviour and her inability to love me as it won't change me! I am able though, to understand and recognise what she had to endure as I was growing up, and how this environment emotionally affected my personality and my developing, difficult relationship with her, and my love for others and myself.

Our mum, because of the lack of support (and other reasons), had an unremitting anger, belligerence and hostility towards my old man, which was consistently and constantly played out in an intense, venomous, verbal manner throughout the entirety of my life. At times, as a child, I was warned in no uncertain terms not to speak to him, take money from him, or to accept a lift to school from him. I did accept all of these things from him because he was my dad, but I was in fear of our mum finding out. On one occasion, The Old Man gave me some money, the old pennies, sixpences and other change, to get some sweets. I was so scared that my mum would find the money in my pocket that before I got home, I lined the coins up in the middle of the pavement like Hansel and Gretel's bread for the school kids to find on their way home, pick up and spend. And they did! Even attending my brother's daughter Kate's funeral with my wife, son, daughter and son-in-law in the car, fifty seven years later, my mum still found a disrespectful remark to blatantly blurt out, directed at me, about my now deceased dad! We were early for the funeral, so I rode around Worcester in the car showing my children some old haunts, and we went past a park where my dad used to clean the toilets as part of his responsibilities as the park keeper. I flippantly remarked 'that's where The Old Man cleaned the shithouse and she quickly quipped 'that's it – shit to shit'! I didn't say anything. I never did. The rest of my family in the car were mortified, but as ever she had the look of contentment and satisfaction that she had yet again attacked him at my expense, but at the expense of my respect and value of her as my mother!

At no time was I ever allowed to forget or disbelieve that The Old Man was a drinker, beater, that he was aggressive or idle, and at no time in my life contributed a penny to my upbringing, and our mum regularly informed me that he never believed I was his child. Our mum was so traumatised by my dad beating her up that when she was pregnant with me she tried to abort me before I was born by taking a red-hot bath! I literally could write a sequel book on the lifelong bitterness she held on to with regards to the Old Man which does nothing to endear herself to me or our relationship. Our mum may have had reason enough for her lifelong wrath, but I didn't ever see any of her accusations or traits exhibited in The Old Man as my father, albeit I can certainly concur he was never there for me, unlike my mum! That's not to say the things my mum constantly chanted didn't happen, but I never witnessed any of that behaviour ever. Even if he was a murderer, he was still The Old Man! Unfortunately for our mum, her anger and frustration surfaced in other parts of her life, but for me, she is still our mum.

Our mum is now in her eighties and, just like my father in those last moments of his life, she is now in need of an arm to hold onto and she needs care, love and attention but just like with The Old Man, I do not know how to give her that love and attention. I don't know how to because no one showed me. I can offer to mow her grass and take her for a meal and make a brief visit, but it is kept brief, so I do not have to listen to further condemnation on why the family don't care about her or communicate with her or help or love her.

This is a letter I am now writing to my parents:

Dear Mum and Dad,
   You both made me the person I am today, and I am truly grateful for who I am.
I have been happy and successful and have
worked hard to achieve business, personal
and relationship successes. I am proud and
grateful of who I am and where I have come
from. This could only have happened with
an eclectic mix of experiences and emotions with and without you both. I
wouldn't change anything. I have a love
and respect for myself, which continue to
evolve and develop, but are a constant
challenge for me to apply. These emotions
seem to be the very foundation bricks you
both seem to have missed out, and this is
why I have to consciously struggle to put
them into practise in my existence.
   You are both so very different and I
wonder who and what personality I would
have had if your relationship had been
different and you had stayed together? The
Old Man never asked for or wanted anything
and was unassuming. He was very independent and never, ever complained. You were
both complete opposites!
   Despite you both divorcing and our
mum's lifelong, damaging debasing of your
character, behaviour and personality, you

later in life almost got back together again, which just conflicted with and contradicted our mum's continuous spats at you, via me. This only undermines the reality or truth of your claim about the person he was! Who knows?

There is a book and a saying – your parents fuck you up! Certainly, we are a product of our parents and I wonder how my children, Beth and Mike, will view or analyse my parenting skills. I wonder how I have fucked them up! We all dive into having children but no one hands us a manual on how to bring them up, do they?

One thing I am genuinely appreciative of and a strong element of my character is that I am grateful and thankful for everything! Not my quote, but how apt. Parenting is as crazy as circumnavigating the globe without a map… but oh, what a journey!

Cliff

So, no father who ever told me he loved me. My mother never told me she loved me or interacted with me, giving no practical guidance. No one ever criticised me, and this not only reinforced my deep and advanced ability to work things out myself but gave me no fear or phobia of failing in the mechanics of life. The more I listened, the more I heard. I was destined to become a politician or businessman, or both with these hard-nosed emotional qualities.

Our mum's second marriage failed and in 1975 I moved away from my home city of Worcester as she married for a 'third time lucky' and I gained two more stepbrothers and a stepsister. I moved to Tenbury and attended a new school for the last six months of my school life.

It was so painful leaving Worcester and all the people and friends I had grown up with, but more agonising was the challenge of changing schools again. I wasn't a great communicator; I found it difficult and was petrified on my first day at my new school at just fifteen. I felt just like that child being dropped at the school gates at the age of five and left to get on with things. All the people at my new school had grown up and been to school with each other since their school life began; friendships and relationships were well formed and here I was – 'Fok'!

Just to make matters worse, my new school had agreed that, as I was only going to be at the school for six months, I could wear my Worcester school uniform, namely a red blazer versus the black blazer of my new school. For Christ's sake, I may as well have also worn a red flashing beacon on my head! This is a person who didn't want to be different or be noticed. Everyone throughout the school was staring at me, particularly in assembly. They were all looking and staring as if I was an extraterrestrial creature or some person with special needs. You couldn't make it up it; it was like a bloody comedy sketch!

I felt so alone again, but I had to pick myself up and make the most of my situation. I was beginning to work on myself, by myself, for myself. It was so painful, but my new class slowly accepted me, and I was being noticed by the girls. The lads were a little apprehensive about me as I was from Worcester and wore Doc Marten boots and spoke funny. This was certainly going to be a character-building period!

My CSE syllabus at Worcester was different to the exam syllabus at Tenbury School, so my results were very poor, and my departing school report read: 'Clifford has not left any lasting impression in his short time with us' and 'untapped ability'!

Forty years later, I helped organise our school reunion, and I did the media work for the event. Again, a bit of humour and a good picture sells the story.

```
TENBURY SCHOOL REUNION FORTY YEARS ON
It was the hottest and driest summer on
record.
    A Minister for Drought was appointed
and in different parts of the country vil-
lages that had disappeared beneath the wa-
ter to create reservoirs came back into
view.
```

It was also the year when a cohort of students was preparing to leave Tenbury High School. Now, forty years on, three of them are turning to the Advertiser for help.

The three former Tenbury School class-mates, Derek James, Cliff Slade and Shaun Drinkwater are calling up former pupils in the class of '76' for a get-together to mark the 40th anniversary of leaving the then, Tenbury Secondary Modern School.

They are planning a get together at Penlu Sports Club on Saturday the eleventh of July at 6 pm and are urging former pupils to get in touch and join them to reminisce the night away.

Derek James, who is organising the event, said they have already been in contact with many past class friends, but some are proving difficult to track down, despite seeking assistance from national Penal establishments!

Cliff Slade is keen for the get-together this year as his comb-over is proving very difficult to maintain into the future, and Shaun Drinkwater remembers that 1976 was infamous for its heatwave and one of the hottest summers ever recorded, when the sun naturally bleached his hair. But he admits that he now needs a little bit of artificial assistance to keep his locks blonde!

Former teachers have also been contacted and are also keen to review the
former students' life progress! Shaun and
Cliff are teaming up to provide some live
music.
All three said the combination of music,
food and, of course, the lifelong bond of
spending all their school years together,
makes for a great evening.

One good friend, in the centre of the school reunion picture, is Shaun Drinkwater. We were in the same class. We organised the reunion with others, we both attended discos and early beer training in the local pubs, later supported each other on the same watch within Hereford and Worcestershire Fire service as fire fighters and came together again playing in a band 'Jake and the Jesters'. It was around this time that Shaun sadly lost his father, which for anyone is an upsetting time. Shaun asked me to pen something for him to read out at his father's church service. I listened to Shaun and put something together for him. As the funeral service date and time approached, Shaun asked me if I would do the address for him and read it out! I was horrified, and my own dad's funeral address experience quickly poured back into my thoughts. The pain was such that I tactfully informed Shaun that for those very reasons, I was not able to do it.

Over the next few days I reflected. I was disappointed in myself and disappointed I was unable to help Shaun in his moment of need. He was the kind of person who would drop anything to help me or others. He was a good friend, and I was upset I had not got the strength to overcome my own fears. I was overwhelmed by being asked to do this, not only for Shaun but for Roy, his dad. What a privilege! What a special responsibility to have the opportunity to say some words that close the curtain on his whole life. I had to put my own experience, my own inhibitions and anxiety to one side and do something. I was petrified and called Shaun and said I would do it – do it for him and do it for me!

This was the address I wrote and delivered at Roy Drinkwater's funeral – my mate's dad. RIP Roy – I did it!

Roy was born in 1936 and he really was the original born and bred Tenbury lad – the family lived in Saltbox Lane and Roy's father, Harold, was a butcher at Bowketts. Roy would often recall how he helped his dad deliver meat in and around Tenbury in a pony and trap, with the meat wrapped in paper and tied together with string. Roy had a brother, Ivor, and a sister, Joan. Roy's mum, Cath, also worked hard to provide and keep the family.

The family soon moved to where most locals seem to originate from – 'up Crescent Place'. Here Roy would be seen in and around the fields playing football with his mates. He was a very good player and would later turn out and play many times for Tenbury United. Roy, at this early age, would also apply his early woodwork skills making bows and arrows and catapults.

Later, Roy's interest in wood further developed, and with the help of his father, he secured an apprenticeship with local builder, John McGrath.

Halfway through his apprenticeship with John McGrath, Roy was called up for national service. Roy enlisted as an infantryman into the King's Shropshire Light Infantry. He served in Germany and unfortunately saw active service in Kenya during the Mau Mau uprising and subsequent conflict. It was this experience that really affected Roy as he, thereafter, would always try and support Kenya and East Africa through charity and aid contributions.

Roy finished his national service and returned home to complete his apprenticeship with John McGrath. And it was around this time that Roy and his mate decided to go for a drink in Ludlow. They went to a pub called The Compasses. It was here that Roy was, for a second time in his life, going to be greatly affected – but *this* time in a different way. There, across the room, was a dark-haired, slender figure in a flowery, dancing frock and wearing high heeled shoes, and it was, of course… John McGrath…

It was, of course, Joyce Bountford, and they immediately fell in love. In Roy's own words 'It was love at first sight'. Their love was so intense that they quickly got married late in 1959 and Shaun was born in early 1960. Roy and Joyce were married for fifty eight years, which is incredible.

In 1967, Roy decided to put a team of tradesmen together and Roy Drinkwater Building was born. The much-respected company built over thirty of some of the finest houses in and around Tenbury. And, of course, Shaun, Jake and Pete still run the family business today.

Anyone who worked for, or with, Roy said that he was a good boss; he was fair, always ready to get stuck in, and was a respected all-round tradesman. Roy always put safety before any job and he was perceived as a caring, decent guy.

Roy was also very principled when it came to paying a fair wage and was also very principled when it came to collecting money for his work. On one occasion, a client, Cleobury Town Council weren't quiet forthcoming with his payment for work done on the town hall, so Roy found a novel way of recovering the debt. Roy's picture appeared on the front page of the Shropshire Star, with Roy holding a set of keys to the locked town hall. The big headline was 'No Cheque – No Keys!' Roy was a great joker, always had a joke, a wicked sense of humour and was always the life and soul of any party or gathering. Roy was a great fan of Tommy Cooper and would often don his fez and do a great impersonation. He loved a drink and was very much a man's man; one of his favourite drinking haunts was the Duke up at Leysters.

But first and foremost, Roy was a family man; he was a much-loved husband, father, grandfather, father-in-law, brother and uncle. If ever there was a family gathering it was, more often than not, at Roy and Joyce's house. His family and getting together was very important to him.

If ever there was a family problem, everybody seemed to go to Roy first. He always listened without being judgemental.

Joyce really was the love of his life, and although they were not in the best of health, every week Roy would make the effort to visit Joyce and spend some time together; they really were devoted and loved each other. Unfortunately and sadly, given Joyce's condition, she can't be here today.

Roy loved equally all of Shaun's wives. Deb and Sue were very close to Roy and they both worked very hard to support and care for him, and Roy was always very grateful to you. Shaun is also sincerely thankful for everything you did for his dad. Roy had an extended granddaughter, Siobhan, and he never left her out and always included her in the family.

Roy was also very grateful and appreciative of his carers at 'Sovereign' and again, Roy and Shaun were very grateful for your dedication and care.

Roy loved his son, Shaun, and of course, Shaun thought the world of his dad. Roy was really a 'hands-on' father and he encouraged Shaun to go out and enjoy himself. In work and life, Roy's style was always to let Shaun carry on and make his own mistakes – of course, those mistakes were then rarely repeated.

Shaun's dad bought him his first set of drums and regularly spent long weekends transporting Shaun around the area giving him the opportunity to play in local bands. Roy loved watching Shaun play in a band and was rightly very proud of him.

The absolute apple of Roy's eye was, of course, his only grandson, Jake. Jake and his grandad were inseparable and really did grow up together and enjoyed precious personal moments right from the start.

I was fortunate to be looking through some old family photographs with Roy on his hands and knees, with a young Jake riding on his back with both of their back ends sticking out of a bush, and they were having great fun which was typical of their relationship.

Jake received the same patience and attention as his dad did when it came to sharing and imparting his carpentry skills. Jake and his grandad last worked together making a beautiful and challenging wooden picture frame which is one of the nicest reminders of spending time with a loved one anyone could ever wish for – something they both crafted together. Once the frame was completed, Roy declared, 'he'll make a chippy'.

Roy was a caring, loving person and when he was really ill in hospital, Shaun and Jake had their chance to say their goodbyes. Roy pulled Jake to one side and said 'Jake, look after your mum and dad'. His last words to Shaun were to look after his mum and his family. Then Roy said to Shaun 'I love you more than the world', and then he hesitated and said, 'no, more than the universe'.

That was the person Roy was - that's the sort of love and care he had for others.

I did it, only just though. I started to break at the end! It was great to have an acknowledgment from Shaun in his thank you notice in the local paper.

DRINKWATER Roy
- The family would like to thank everyone for attending the funeral service, for the donations received and for all the messages of sympathy and support. Also, a huge thank you to the British Legion Choir, who were absolutely wonderful, and to Clifford Slade for the address.'

I left school in 1976, and at sixteen I went to the university of life at 'Wells Soft Drinks', a local bottling factory straight in as a 'general operative'. One thing resonated within my psyche at that time and that was the time I went to collect my overalls. I was told that once I put those overalls on, I would never take them off again! Distinctly, I remember climbing into them with a little reflection of how sad that would be, as some of my friends were going to college, university or into office jobs. I was to spend the next eighteen years at the pop factory which was an incredible, fantastic journey which I would not have changed for the world. One day I will write a book about Wells Soft Drinks and my experiences and knowledge that I attained throughout my time there.

Although eighteen years was a long time to work at a factory, always in my mind was the thought regarding climbing into the overalls. Initially, I admired my supervisors and superiors. In the first couple of years, I just exercised my greatest skills and attributes. I listened, watched and learnt. I always looked up to people in management and put them on a pedestal and was in awe of their confidence and ability to write, present and organise, and of how educated they were. However, I always knew I could do better than them, irrespective of their education, experience or knowledge. I watched inferior individuals being promoted in a fast developing and expanding company – inferior in my eyes from the perspective that I could do a better job than them. I knew how because I did, because I observed, and the more I looked, the more I saw and the more I listened, the more I heard. Because I worked things out myself on my own, I could understand how to do things differently, better and for the greater good. I was just lacking an important link in my nature... confidence! Each week, month and year I was gaining confidence. I was being accepted as one of the boys in the factory. I was splitting my time with my new friends in Tenbury and my old world in Worcester. I wasn't quite ready to let go of Worcester. I was starting to get interested in girls and they were noticing me. After my first year in my green overalls, I was seventeen and started my driving lessons, and at the second attempt I passed and bought my first car, a Vauxhall Viva PCJ 188G out of my earnings! I had many female brief encounters at this time which I kept brief because I was not physically mature enough to take a relationship any further and girls scared me to death for that reason. The girls were very forward – bloody 'eck!

Here is a letter to myself with that time firmly in my mind!

Dear Cliff,
    I am enjoying myself so much at work. The money is amazing. I love my job and have just saved up enough to buy my own car. Driving and being independent and able to go when and where I like are amazing. Although it is illegal, I even have a CB. My handle is 'Joey'. The smell of the factory is fantastic. The pungent odour of freshly imported commute oranges, lemons, blackcurrants and limes are as if I was walking in the fresh fields or orchards,

as is the clanking of the bottles on the production line. I could even hear the clanking in bed at night as I went off to sleep. I really want to drive a stacker truck and load the lorries like all the other lads. I will drive a truck.

Home is a bit difficult at the moment: three boys, Nigel, Shaun and me and three girls Pauline, Tracey and Jude. With the addition of our mum and Derek, home at times, in a three-bedroom semi-detached house, is not only tight, but tense and fraught! I really feel for Tracey and Shaun as they seem to be getting the sharp end of my mother's and Derek's new relationship - it's not good! Apart from home, bloody girls want to go out with me at the discos. Mentally and, certainly from a fantasy element, I am ready for them, but physically and biologically with two hairs on my chin, I'm not quite ready for them yet!

I have now had what I can call my first girlfriend. This lasted a fair few months and I was still with my mates at Worcester. One evening in Worcester, I gave a girl a lift home as she was probably the most attractive girl on the whole of the Warndon estate in Worcester at the time. As she got out of the car she said 'by the way, I really fancy you' and gave me a clever wink! I think what she really meant was 'by the way, I really fancy your car!' I then had a serious girlfriend that lasted even many more months. She complemented the now six hairs on my chin and five hairs each side of my wiener! With this girl on my semi-hairy arms and money in my pocket and the go-faster wheel spins on my car, my confidence and ego were starting to grow in more places than one! My mates were in awe and I thought I was the boy. It was the hottest period in the history of recorded weather, as well as my adolescent life!

Apart from home, life is good. Life is bloody good! Life is now, enjoy it, embrace it and grow through it. Every day we get a new chance, a new experience, a new hope and an exciting anticipation. It's called, tomorrow! Tomorrow is also a new hair!

Cliff Slade – getting hairy and loving
my overalls 1976/7

Although I was under the umbrella of the Wells Drinks bottling factory, every year or other year, great things happened to me from a work and personal development. Every step of the way I also learnt to write letters of applications, or later in various supervisory, management roles. This was the beginning of my letter writing, which up until now, was always done for me by my mum as I was incapable of writing a letter. I moved from a factory operative to a machine operator, then to a forklift driver, shift charge hand, shift supervisor, assistant warehouse manager, and warehouse manager. I had stepped out of those green overalls and I had a tie, a white coat and white hat. I kept walking past the clocking-in clock where the staff notice board was, with a notice written by me, informing staff of their holiday entitlement, signed by Cliff Slade – Warehouse Manager. It was also underlined. I was now on a salary and working days, and I was the bollocks to be fair. I was good at my job because of all that observation and listening as a child, which I could now turn into practice! I didn't suffer fools. I was now impatient; I was in overdrive and I never got burnt by the same flame twice. I wanted more for myself.

Always running beside my work life was my family; I always did something to challenge myself in a volunteer role; I always wanted to give; and giving feels good. I wanted to experience life and the role of the police, so I joined up as a special police constable and served for five years in Tenbury, Ludlow and Leominster. I loved, and developed during my time in the police, and made some lifelong friends in the service. As well as the thorough training, and on-the-job experience, it was a massive eye-opener for me, and I gained some life experiences, skills and knowledge, that I was able to apply in other situations, both in my life then and now. The experience of racing around in a police car to emergency incidents with blue lights and sirens blaring, whilst trying to feed information back on a crackling radio to headquarters and on to the ground colleagues was exhilarating. Attending street and pub fights, arresting individuals or trying to defuse situations in domestic incidents or bereavement circumstances by accident, self-inflicted or suspicious means, were all experienced along with traffic control and foot patrol really testing my character to its maximum. I loved every minute and was becoming an individual no one back on the streets of my home city in Worcester would recognise. I was different and growing and changing! I was the only person responsible for my success. Failure wasn't an option, and everything was happening for a reason. I trusted myself and I knew more than I thought I knew. Everything I wanted to do, I did it, and I always wanted to do or try something different. Life is for living and experiencing, and I made myself priority. I was always happy, I was always *genuinely* happy. I was always successful because I was always happy. Happiness is the key to success. I was both and still am – I always am! Some comedians are depressives at home; some happy people are miserable at home. I'm not, I'm genuinely always happy. What you see is what I am! I keep repeating, I'm always grateful. Being grateful is the beginning of happiness and I'm always grateful.

After five years in the police service, I changed blue lights and joined Hereford and Worcester Fire Service. I drove an eleven-tonne fire appliance for eleven years and formed a lifelong camaraderie with a further group of people, as well as accruing further character-changing experiences, skills and knowledge. The fire service had a saying – 'keep one hand on the ladder for the brigade and one hand for your family'. That is so true and hopefully that is how life, in general, should be. One hand to help yourself and one hand to help others!

The Fire Service also developed my sense and everyone else's sense of humour; it is communally and commonly known as a dark sense of humour. As fire fighters, we would generate amusing anecdotes out of desperately tragic situations, experiences, or near misses. Collectively, or one to one, this is how we would deal with unbearable and unthinkable circumstances. Also, within two fire crews of six covering our area, the humour and mocking between individuals and watches were constant and not for the faint-hearted. 'Piss-taking' was intense, but we all looked out for and protected each other in times of need in the job or outside of the job, and never joked on the job. If you were unwittingly drawn into its grasp, humour was also silly, sophisticated, and unbelievable at times. One such time which incorporated all three, I let my guard down and fell victim to probably the worst joking individual on red watch, Shaun Drinkwater. Our alerters went off and we all rushed to the station. I grabbed the number two tally, which defined me as the driver, and Bengi Brittain was assigned tally number one, which is the officer in charge position in the front seat next to me. Four other crew members were quickly boarding in the back compartment, and I noticed Shaun Drinkwater in the corner of my eye so I knew we had a good, experienced and capable crew. The station door flung open, blue lights lit up the bright daylight, and the sirens howled. All other road users cleared the way, my heart was thumping, the adrenalin was flooding my body, and I gasped to catch my breath and bring my body and mind under control in order that I could safely get this fire appliance and its occupants safely to the location to deal with the incident; time was of the essence and it was take-off time. We screeched off towards Cleobury Mortimer. The emergency call was a road traffic collision, and we needed to get there quickly. The Cleobury Mortimer road was very challenging to negotiate as it was narrow, bendy, hilly and thwarted by agricultural and conventional traffic.

My Emergency Fire Appliance Driving (EFAD) training immediately kicked in, and I was focused on making progress to this incident, safely, quickly and in one piece as other road users paved the way, at times orderly, but most of the time disorderly and unpredictably as an eleven-tonne fire appliance screamed behind and in front of them. As we made progress, Bengi, as the officer in charge, was dealing with the radio and gathering more instructions and information. The rear crew were frantically, and always with great difficulty in a cramped rear crew compartment, trying to get dressed into fire kit as the fire engine turned and bumped the crew from side to side and up and down as if on an expensive amusement park ride! We had cleared take off. Everyone was dressed and the crew were now respectfully quiet as I was now the centre of focus speedily advancing towards Cleobury. This was a difficult drive considering the challenging route and the alternating speed required to negotiate this awful road. I was considered a good driver; my reputation was good and I could handle the appliance confidently being a well-seasoned driver, and we were going very fast to this incident. The crew in the back were now getting fidgety and nervous at the pace we were now gathering. Speed was always everyone else's secret worry because after all, we all wanted to arrive in one piece, albeit quickly. To break the nervous silence, Shaun popped his head over my shoulder and said, 'put your foot down'. Everyone laughed and subconsciously I increased my pace. Shaun then did the same again and blurted out, 'this is a blue-light job you know – you want to hurry up!' Everyone laughed again which caused me to respond by increasing the pressure on the accelerator, resulting in the appliance going even faster. At that very moment and without any warning, a car appeared in front and approached me in the middle of the road – a road too narrow for the fire appliance and the other vehicle to pass each other without a head on collision. Very quickly, I responded by taking evasive action and dramatically swerved to avoid the almost inevitable crash, and we all jerked to the left and the appliance left the road. I braced myself with gritted teeth awaiting the carnage and impact that were about to be inflicted upon us. With a huge bump and thud, the fire engine left the carriageway and came to a sudden halt. We were resting up against a telegraph pole and, as Bengi's window was open, his face and cheek were squashed up against the pole. There was a clattering and struggling noise coming from the rear compartment as the four rear passengers were recovering and uncoupling themselves from being on top of each other. Shaun popped his head over to me again, with his helmet now skewed on the side of his head and in a loud voice said, 'you want to slow down you stupid prat!' Thankfully and miraculously no one, nor the appliance, were any the worse for our lucky escape, and we all laughed for many years thereafter about this and many, many other close calls on call!

True to form and needing a new challenge albeit, eleven years later, I left the fire service and applied, and was successful, in being selected as a magistrate, a 'justice of the peace', in my home city of Worcester. As I write this, I am in my sixteenth year in this position, so my rush to live life is slowing down, as far as doing something different is concerned!

As well as working hard and enjoying being successful in work and within volunteer roles, I also learnt to play bass guitar and played in a band 'Total Recall'.

In work and in life, outside of family, I met certain individuals to whom I am eternally grateful; people who give something of themselves for no other reason than they are genuine, nice and sincere, and they have left a positive footprint on my character. Again, being thankful is so important to me. When someone gives something of himself for no reason other than that mentioned above, it is special, and it is difficult for me to accept or comprehend. I always gave of myself easily; giving for me is my way of showing I care and saying thank you, and also to show my love. My letter 'great experience on election trail' later in this book explains how I felt in my letter of thanks and sums up how humbling it is to accept from others and what this means to me. However, the pain is almost embarrassingly difficult for me personally. When someone gives to me, it is almost unbearable. Later in life, I was taught to embrace and accept this, but it's still strange and uncomfortable even today – strange and uncomfortable to me, because I give to show someone affection and love – I help them in any way I can. So, I cannot accept that they are showing me love and affection in this way and thus I reject it.

One of those individuals I would do anything for, or give anything to, is a guy called Trevor Jones, who taught me to play bass guitar and never asked for a penny. He spent hours with me, never gave up on me, and was always there encouraging me. He is a talented musician who is a personal hero of mine, and I cannot speak more highly of him for embracing me and taking me under his musical wing – Total Recall. Trevor, John Greenhouse and I were together for over four years, which is an incredible amount of time for an amateur band to be with each other. We played locally and further afield as a tight popular band, and it was an amazing experience. It petrified me stepping onto stage every time. What a stepping stone in my personal growth from the age of seventeen to twenty two, but it had to be done and I had to do it! Trevor and John were the first people to embrace me for no reason. They chose me as a friend, but I also chose them. I chose them because they were doers and believers. I was attracted to them and they were attracted to me, and they could see something in me – I was bloody handsome though! I always thought I was good looking! At no time did I ever think I was good or the best at playing bass guitar, but if I didn't believe I was the best, I pretended I was, and then I was – it's easy. I was then, and still am, 'the great pretender'! Some Shakespeare guy said:

All the world's a stage,
And all the men and women merely players;

They have their exits and their entrances,
And one man in his time plays many parts…

Such was my bond with John Greenhouse that he was later to become my best man because he was the best man!

One other person I learnt from, who again formed so much of my character, was a military woman who was, much later, my boss at Wells Soft Drinks, Christine Beedles. She identified me as a rising management star and promoted me several times, and sent me on regular training, development and management courses, which also greatly fast-tracked my writing and presentation skills. She really was my mentor, management mother and working relationship guru. When she left the company, I too was ready to fledge, spread my wings and fly out of the security of employment, and into entrepreneurship space. I was ready to start up my own first business. Again, I knew everything. I was so powerful in myself. I had no fears, I had no barriers or slightest doubt, I had a clear vision of success and I could see it. It was the only thing I could see. I didn't think outside the box because I didn't understand what that meant, so there was no box. I was raring to go and I was a doer, not a dreamer. After all, I could make things happen from an early age. No one criticised me, no one noticed me, no one bothered with me, but it was now time for me to step up and be noticed.

Who for? No one – I wanted to do it for me. I wanted to be me for me, and the best I could be!

The minute I decided to think up and start my business, I knew instinctively what to do. It did not matter what the business was. I knew I had to do something the same, only differently. For example, if I was delivering milk (a milkman), I had to think how to deliver milk the same but in a different way, like in plastic bags rather than bottles.

Starting a business, from marketing, managing, delivering and getting customers, was just like everything I had done and everything I still had to do and was to come. It was little letters. I was good at little letters. Little letters were defining my life. Jigsaw pieces make a puzzle, a completed puzzle forms a picture! Life is little pieces – little letters become stories, stories become books!

I decided to use my knowledge and experience as a materials handling instructor to start a materials handling training company 'Transport Training Services', offering training courses into industry. I started writing letters to attract clients. Those letters formed my business.

Firstly, I would ring a company up to find out who was responsible for materials handling training. The receptionist was the gatekeeper to keep me away from the person I needed to talk to; they were good at preventing people like me talking to these very busy managers and directors who already had a training provider, and they didn't want to talk to me. But I was better than them, and nine times out of ten, I got through to the person I needed to impress, but more importantly, to engage with, form a relationship with quickly, and just be me. That, in turn, relaxed them. People sell to people!

'Good morning, how are you? Have you had a good weekend? Wow, it's cold today!' Being normal, being natural, being polite and being respectful were endearing. That was my first hurdle. Balance was also important – too nice, or not nice enough, could blow my chance to identify the person that I wanted to speak to.

'Who is the person I can send some details to about our materials handling training service we provide?' I am not asking to speak to them yet, and the gatekeeper is happy to continue engaging with me. I get their name and delve a little more! 'what is their job title, just so it's correct in the post?'

Now this was the big bombshell! 'could you just put me through to 'A.N. Other' and I'll let them know I'm sending something in the post?' – 'yes,' they would retort, 'I'll put you through.'

I would then repeat the whole process, but this time with the 'decision maker'. I had written and produced an amazing 'different' and 'better' brochure than all my competitors, and it really was an eye-catcher! They would remember it and they would remember me!

My covering letter was just another letter with the brochure:

Dear A.N. Other,

Further to our telephone conversation today, please find enclosed our brochure and information on Transport Training Services detailing the service we can provide A&N Other Ltd.

Transport Training Services is an ITS-SAR accredited training company. We have 75 instructors strategically located throughout the UK, who all appear on the ITSSAR register of approved instructors, and they are all fully qualified and experienced on the machines they give instruction on. All our courses are recognised by The Health & Safety Executive through our accreditation.

Transport Training Services conducts all training on customer premises only; this allows us to train in a flexible and practical manner, and can accommodate within normal shift working patterns.

Our customers range from local wholesalers and small manufacturers with simple basic requirements, right through to major manufacturing, retailing, warehousing and cargo handling companies with multiple depots across the UK.

We offer a fixed rate (per day, max 3 delegates per course). There are no hidden charges for weekends or shifts (excluding night shift. This attracts a small premium on our daily rate).

As discussed, I will contact you in a couple of days to see if we can be of any assistance to you in the future. If you require any more information, please do not hesitate to contact me. In the meantime, assuring you of our best attention.

Kind regards,

Cliff Slade
Transport Training Services

Within a week, whilst fresh in their mind, I called them and was put straight through to them. I made an appointment and the new customer was bagged!

I regularly put press releases out and potential clients wanted to be part of a successful emerging company – 'success breeds success' although it was fake news! But those under pressure, namely journalists, were eager for a story and a picture if it was one less piece that they had to go out and seek.

A press release was just another letter really. It's what I did. I wrote letters and an attractive picture was always supplied. The picture was in my head and I always used the same photographer, Jeremy Pardoe. I knew what

I wanted and we always jelled, and Jeremy was a seasoned press photographer.

These three press releases represented five years of start, middle and end of one business, and then I started again with a new business.

COMPANY GROWS AND TURNOVER DOUBLES

A Tenbury Wells-based company has strengthened its commercial activities with the recruitment of a new Commercial Manager.

Gary Haworth has been given the role of commercial manager at Transport Training services (UK) Ltd, a materials training company.

During the past two years the company has grown and turnover has doubled.

It has recently relocated to Teme Street, Tenbury Wells, and has an administrative team of six, plus 24 instructors across the country.

Gary joins the company at a very successful time,' said Cliff Slade, head of the operation.

Gary brings with him a wealth of experience and will be targeting specific industries to increase Transport Training Services' market share and build on its continued growth and success', said Matthew Ewan, who is responsible for the company's national commercial strategies.

ALL SMILES AT TENBURY BASED TRANSPORT

TRAINING SERVICES

Left to right: Lorraine Houchin, Deb Marston, Cliff Slade, Debby Gatehouse, Julie Slade.

Tenbury Wells-based Transport Training Services are all smiles after landing one of the country's biggest, single material handling training contracts.

Leamington Spa-based Waxely UK, a national distributor of plumbing and heating products and a supplier of construction materials, has extended its existing agreement with TTA for a further two years.

TTA Managing Director Cliff Slade said, 'This is a huge boost for TTA in a climate of uncertainty and weakening markets. This news gives us the confidence to further invest, not only in our team in Tenbury, but also to further invest in improving our market share. We are delighted and this result is testament to the hard work and dedication everyone here consistently delivers.'

Waxely UK Health, Safety & Environmental Operations Manager said, 'Waxely's vast branch network requires its forklift, crane and lorry driver training provider to offer a flexible and quality service across the whole of the UK. TTA provides such a service.

'Waxely's dedication to providing excellent health and safety standards requires providers to meet stringent performance targets and Transport Training consistently achieves these requirements.'

We always had a great laugh - I had the picture slightly edited - not for the press, just for the office amusement!

Lorraine always enjoyed her food and from time to time would spill food down her front, so I gave her a bib, a knife and fork and a plate of nosh! For some reason it was a joke that Deb had a little head (pin head) so I shrank her head! Julie's boobs were proportioned to give her a voluptuous front! Deb was finance so she was very close to me, so I changed her into a parrot on my shoulder.

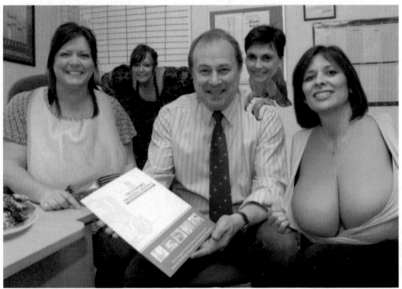

Later, I sold the business and started again. I built up two training companies and successfully sold them. My motivation and excitement were starting the business and building it up. Once it was successful, I lost interest in it and moved on! My businesses and my interests and my life were all like letters. I could only act, write and be interested in short stories and then I started again! Time for another letter!

NEW CHIEF AIMING TO CREATE JOBS
New jobs are expected following changes at Tenbury-based Transport Training Services

and the future looks bright for the company.

Local businessman, Cliff Slade, the current manager director, is standing down after five years at the helm of what has been one of the largest independently owned materials handling training providers in the country.

When his former employer of eighteen years, Wells Soft Drinks, decided to relocate to another part of the country, Cliff started his own business in the spare room of his home address with humble aspirations of just paying himself a salary.

Five years later Transport Training Services have a £1m turnover, a head office team of five in town and some thirty five instructors located throughout the UK.

Cliff said: 'the business has and continues to boom beyond expectations. It is now time to hand over the baton to ensure the company, not only maintains its strong market position, but also has the vision and leadership in becoming the leading materials handling training provider in the United Kingdom.'

New managing director, Mr Colin Brent, a former director with Brendon Pipes, said: 'The company head office will not only remain in Tenbury Wells but also has plans to extend its administration and marketing functions which would lead to further jobs.

'Cliff Slade has built some solid foundations over the past five years and I look forward to maintaining the growth.'

For Cliff, 41, it is not quite retirement. He has some other business interests which he will be developing outside of the training industry.

I then formed a new company, Transport Training Agency, and repeated the whole process again, only even better and differently.

The second time in business I changed my management style. I still had the force, drive and ambition to be successful but gone was the need to be a leader, gone was the need to be responsible and be in control, gone was my ego, gone was my need to influence and be powerful or dominant. I had been there, done that, and I wanted to lead differently! I handed the responsibility to the people who worked for me. I let them take time off when they wanted, go shopping when they wanted, start late, finish early to suit them, go on Facebook, do online shopping and select their own staff. They organised regular staff outings, all fully funded by the company. If we worked hard, we would go for pub lunches. I closed down at Christmas, paid a bonus as well as an excellent salary. All

I asked was for them to do their jobs to the best of their ability, and they did fantastic jobs. Not one of them had a day off sick, and we had excellent customer relations, as well as content, supportive, committed, motivated staff. Letting others take responsibility, giving them responsibility and allowing others to grow and develop without any rules or constraints, were a massive success and the news below was a testament to that style.

CELEBRATION FOR TENBURY TRAINING COMPANY
Materials handling training and driving assessment company, Transport Training Agency based in Tenbury Wells are celebrating the confirmation as sole training provider for one of the country's biggest building supply merchants. Cliff Slade, Managing Director, commented that this million pound contract is great news for the current staff based at Tenbury and is an additional springboard for further investment and growth in the company.

Cliff added that 'our operations office at St Helens has recently been relocated to Tenbury, and this coupled with the confirmation of our new Operations Manager, Tim Brookes, has completed the first part of this investment and the future looks good.' He continued, 'Tim will be heading our operation and he comes to us with a successful and strong track record of logistics and distribution management background. Tim's experience and knowledge will complement our current management team and we have an aggressive agenda for further development.'

Transport Training Agency has thirty two material handling instructors located throughout the UK, and they are supported by nine Driving Standard Agency qualified driving instructors who carry out driver assessments for its corporate clients.

Tim is very much looking forward to his new role, and added that with three Health & Safety supported accreditation marks RTITB, ITSSAR and LANTRA, Transport Training Agency are not only able to offer a broad range of training courses, but also quality, professional and industry recognised qualifications anywhere in the UK.

I then sold the company with a huge contract in place just as the international, crippling markets crashed. Phew! What a complete master timing stroke! I sold for peak money within a diminishing and shrinking business climate. I was the one who saw it coming. I worked hard on the sale and I drove the sale to a successful conclusion with a 1.2 million turnover.

It was now time for something completely different but again my drive was a new business venture. The format was the same, exactly the same: self-belief, determination and don't talk about doing something or dream about doing something, do it! I had no fear and didn't ever think anything I did would fail because, as that child, no one took any notice of me. I worked things out myself. I did it my way by simply listening and then doing it! If you have been successful once you will be successful again and I was.

TENBURY BUSINESSMAN CLIFF MEDIATES
Tenbury businessman Cliff Slade is in the business of resolving disputes.

An emerging Tenbury-based mediation company Team Mediation Ltd., has added a number of new mediation elements to its portfolio of services.

Managing director, Cliff Slade, said its core business involved matrimonial and disputes within the family, but there are many other areas where mediation can help.

'A breakdown of a family relationship can be very upsetting and can at times lead to days, months and sometimes years of no contact,' he said.

'Over time these matters lead to worry and serious health issues if left unresolved, just because of a misunderstanding or an argument.

'Family mediation really is an opportunity to give all parties a voice and allows individual family members involved to work out their own way of moving forward in, at times, a very sensitive area.'

He said that the benefit of mediation is that it is likely to be much less expensive or acrimonious than going down a legal path.

'The biggest barriers to people sorting things out are emotion and pride and a mediator can often help address these issues,' said Cliff Slade.

I just kept inventing stories and news and it, in turn, attracted customers and clients. People wanted to be part of good news and a successful business. You see and you are! Writing an article was free advertising – an article was just another letter.

MEDIATION FIRM EXTENDS ITS RANGE OF

SERVICES

Mediator Cliff Slade, managing director of Team Mediation

Rather than rush to the courts, an increasingly popular way of settling family disputes these days is by mediation.

And now Worcestershire based mediation company, Team Mediation Ltd, has added a number of new mediation elements to its portfolio of services.

Cliff Slade, managing director of the Tenbury Wells-based firm, said its core business was still within the matrimonial sector, but other family disputes such as arguments between mothers, fathers, siblings and all other family relationships were now very much areas where help was being sought.

He added: 'a breakdown of a family relationship can be very upsetting and can at times lead to days, months and sometimes years of no contact. Over time these matters lead to worry and serious health issues if left unresolved, just because of a misunderstanding or an argument. Family Mediation really is an opportunity to give all parties a voice and allows individual family members involved to work out their own way of moving forward in, at times, a very sensitive area.

Mr Slade said other services developing in the sector included community mediation, which deals with disputes between neighbours, friends etc., and school mediation where parents and schools do not agree on some issues affecting their child's education, such as behaviour, progress, relationships etc. Team Mediation can be contacted via www.team-mediation.co.uk.

It did not matter what I chose to do from a business perspective because I could always make money. We can all make money if we believe, visualise and do it, but do it differently, offer something extra to what others are offering – be better. 'Do it!' are the two biggest words in my vocabulary. I hear every single day, family, friends and acquaintances say 'I am going to start my own business'. 'I have an idea for a new business.' 'I am going to make a fortune!' And that is about how far most people get with starting a business. We can all talk a good business, but it takes that risk, that fear, that courage, that drive, that determination, that visualisation, that belief, without thinking of the obstacles or 'what ifs'.

I studied and listened how other companies, traders or businesses did things and then I did it the same – only differently and better. I was always that child, that child who listened with my ears and eyes open and my mouth shut. That's why we have two ears and one mouth. My next business was just a taxi in a small town.

What did I do differently then? I listened to the competition and customers, and studied the competition. All I had to do in this instance was to be polite, friendly, respectful, courteous and caring – everything people were telling me my competitors were not! Also, very important was not to overcharge, but more importantly, not to undercharge. People, customers and clients will always be suspicious of a bargain. Within three years, this business was turning over £85k - £85k of my competitors' business! Time for a letter. I could call myself an entrepreneur now!

Pictured: Leader of Malvern Hills District Council Phil Grove with Cliff Slade and John Moore

Tenbury Wells businessman and entrepreneur, Cliff Slade, is hoping his third business project in the town will be as successful as his previous ventures.

Cliff has identified an opportunity in Tenbury Wells for a professional, competitive private hire vehicle company. Cliff said, 'Tenbury Wells under Malvern Hills District Council has not got its own registered cab company. We are well served with companies in neighbouring Shropshire and Herefordshire but Tenbury Wells, under our local licensing office, has not got a town-based registered vehicle or vehicles'. Cliff added that, 'this is a void, and a service I am keen to offer in the town and the surrounding districts.'

Although Cliff's new enterprise has only been operating since late November, he said 'demand has been terrific, and we are already planning on expanding with additional drivers' jobs being created. The future is indeed looking good with demand increasing week on week'.

Leader of Malvern Hills District Council Phil Grove welcomed this new venture and congratulated Cliff in providing Tenbury with a private hire registered vehicle. Councillor Grove said, 'Cliff is a well-seasoned businessman, who for a decade has been a well-established member of our local commerce, and I wish him all the very best in this new project with this additional service to our community.'

I was always looking for a different challenge, a new experience, a new skill and something to enlighten me. Something I feared, and something that the child who couldn't speak, could never imagine to be. I dared myself to dare!

TENBURY WELLS, BUSINESSMAN CLIFF JOINS
WORCESTER CITY BOARD

A Tenbury businessman has achieved his goal of becoming a director at Worcester City Football Club.

After four decades on the terraces, Cliff Slade was elected to the board by shareholders at the club's annual meeting.

Slade is the managing director of Tenbury-based Transport Training Agency Ltd.

He is looking forward to the challenges that lie ahead at the Blue Square South outfit.

Slade says, 'it is an important time for Worcester City with some of the biggest and most crucial decisions being made in the club's history'.

Worcester City recently submitted plans for a new £6 million, 6,000-seater stadium at Nunnery Way in Worcester.

Slade added that, with his longstanding relationship with the club as a supporter, he was happy to help the board with his knowledge and energy.

In the meantime, I was also enjoying writing letters – letters perhaps to help others. Helping others in any way feels good, even if it is just a simple message. Spreading positivity feels good. A letter can be uplifting and that is all I can write – I can't write a complaint. What's the point? I can't be negative because I don't know how to be negative. I wrote this letter and it went to press to give a foot up for a moment for my nephew. It made him feel good, and me. It was an uplifting success story, a pacey and light-hearted letter. I can write that sort of correspondence because that is who I am!

WORCESTER NEWS, LETTERS: HE DOES A WORLD
CLASS BURGER

Sir - Worcester News (1st July 2017),

I read with interest your culinary article entitled 'Rising, Burger Chef Joins Conservatory'.

It really is an achievement that can only be applauded that this humble, small-time, lay-by snack trailer has been nurtured and developed by local Worcester lad, Carl Sampson into the most popular burger place in Worcester.

It's no small wonder being mentored by Daniel Clifford that 'Sampson's' is now launching a restaurant and delivery service within 'The Conservatory' in the heart of Worcester's eatery quarter.

On Saturday, first of July 2017, I attended Hereford's first food festival and unbeknown to me as I walked onto the multi food arena, there was the big guy himself in his trailer, despatching attractive and smell-bounding burgers to his followers.

We walked around the festival and observed incredible delicacies on offer, but with your weekend piece fresh in my mind, I was drawn back to the Worcester burger warrior and joined the queue.

I'm not really a burger person but my 'Sampson' burger was absolutely mouth-watering – with his acclaimed home-made burger being the main feature which was so tender and tasty.

It was cleverly layered with a secret sauce and a delicious garnish of cheese, spinach, red onion and tomato, and all presented professionally in a light soda bread bap – wow!

Good luck, Carl Sampson! I, for one, can only echo Daniel Clifford's description of his burgers: 'World-class'.

Cliff Slade
Tenbury Wells

In my quest to always do, experience and personally grow, I applied to become a magistrate in 2002. Surely, I couldn't do that could I? Not a bloody magistrate! I did, and I still am, sixteen years later. The initial interview process was challenging, as the selection process was a series of tests over three appointments at various court buildings across the county. I was tested on making structured decisions and collective decision-making, and this came naturally to me. I was naturally inclusive in coming to a decision. I was a natural at listening and deciding on the facts whilst excluding the emotions. Emotions were an easy element to exclude because emotion was an element excluded in my DNA construction. Part of being a manager in my jobs and in business was being ruthless and getting on with things and making things happen. They didn't need emotions! That loveless child experience helped me and defined my business, job and extracurricular activities, but not my personal relationships! I always performed well and enjoyed interviews because I was talking about myself. I was an expert on me and it was an opportunity to share and talk about me which, as a child, was something I didn't do. I didn't speak to anyone so now I was going to tell everybody about me, and I was good at it. After all, no one knew who I was because I didn't tell anyone.

I got the job. I always did if I had an interview. I interviewed well because as in business, I did and said something better and different because I had no boundaries. I was truthful, honest and just me; me was the only gauge I had! I wanted to do it because I feared it. Anything I feared I had to do. I had to do it, and I always did. I wasn't that child anymore and I didn't want to sit, listen and watch the world go by. I wanted to be in the world and fully participating in the world. I proved I could do anything and achieve all I wanted to do because I believed I could – nobody ever told me I couldn't! I was a natural cognitive behavioural therapist (CBT) to myself. I could put things into perspective and flip them over and turn a negative thought into a positive action within that dynamic thought moment. I could do anything, and nobody could or would stop me! In my role as a magistrate, in the early days, I was petrified on my way into court and then I thought – I shouldn't be petrified. I am not the defendant; it's they who should be petrified. I'm making a decision about them, not them about me, so I wasn't scared anymore. CBT!

Thinking someone is going to rumble me and say, 'what are you doing up there?', was always a thought and one day in court that became a reality, and the red face that I was normally able to control unfortunately became a flashing red beacon in a packed court house. I walked into court and everyone respectfully rose to their feet according to court protocol. I then bowed my head and other court professionals returned the traditional exchange with a 'good morning your worship'. The female defendant was brought to her feet and asked to identify herself by the legal advisor. I looked up after she had said her name and date of birth, straight into the eyes of a past, fleeting girlfriend from my Warndon council estate early life! One of my first serious kisses and a little bit more. OMG, OMG, OMG, OMG! My heartbeat immediately quadrupled, my face started to flush, and we looked at each other eye-to-eye for what seemed like forever, and the voices I should have been tuned into, were just a muffled, distant noise. I was not hearing. She was asked to sit down and listen to the charges being put before her. She sat down and broke off eye communication. She, she, she, she, she, she hadn't bloody recognised me. I kept my eyes down pretending to write and read documents in front of me. My heart was still thumping in my chest and my face was still very warm, but I think the forty years' gap had rescued my worst nightmare – phew! She was then asked to stand again by the legal advisor and our eyes locked together again. The legal advisor said to her, 'you have heard the charges before you, how do you plead?' Our eyes were still locked together and the busy court was silently poised for her plea. There was a long lapse and she then clearly replied directly to me, "ere Slabber, is that you?' I was mortified and was completely paralysed from the throat to my lips. 'Slabber' was my Warndon nickname which I hadn't heard for forty plus years! I wanted the floor to open up and engulf me. 'It is you, Slabber, isn't it?' The whole court started to uncomfortably fidget, with a couple of sniggers and smiles, and all-round amusement at this undignified hitch in formal proceedings. I was still in a state of paralysis when she then said, 'hey Slabber, you've done well for yourself. I would not have recognised you in that suit'. This not only upped the amusement, but also brought the Crown Prosecution Service, defence and legal advisor to broad smiles at my inability to function. Quickly, I gestured to the clerk towards me to declare an interest. The clerk said this was a not guilty plea and a trial date-fixing was the only process so therefore, I was not expected to withdraw from the court or this case. This former, semi-love acquaintance, bless her, waved at me as she left the court and said, 'see you, Slabber'. This was of great amusement in the retiring room thereafter, for many years, and still gets brought up many years later as my darkest moment. Sadly, this girl later went on to commit suicide, leaving a young family. RIP and thanks for the memory, in more ways than one!

In my role as a magistrate, I was able to put a few school communication ghosts to bed because I attended various schools as a mentor magistrate in local school Mock Trial Competitions, presenting and talking as a class leader rather than that mute child of early years. Yet another fear still felt but now exorcised. Yet another stepping stone in my journey. As well as something else to write a story about – just another letter!

LONG ARM OF THE LAW AT SCHOOL NEAR TENBURY
Children from a school near Tenbury have been visited by the long arm of the law.

Brayburn Church of England Primary School pupils were on their best behaviour when a police officer and a magistrate attended their class for the afternoon.

Bethany Fernihough, who teaches the class, invited the legal duo in to meet the children as they had spent the term studying the children's chosen project of 'crime and punishment'.

Cliff Slade, a magistrate for 15 years at Worcester and Kidderminster Magistrates' Court, talked and took questions on the role of the magistrate, and PC Mark Brunswick brought in his police equipment for the children to talk about, as well as discussing his role as a police officer.

The children's work included a comprehensive wall display of pastel court paintings in the style of Pricilla Coleman.

Victorian era punishments were explored such as children being sent to prison, as well as witches punished by ducking, right up to today's police investigations with the children making e-fits and fingerprints.

Court role-play and mock trials were also enacted in the classroom.

TENBURY HIGH SCHOOL 'MOCK TRIAL COMPETITION'

Tenbury High School, year eight and nine students, for the second year, entered the County heat of the Mock Trial Competitions held at Worcester Magistrates' Court.

Thirteen schools from across the county took part in the competition, with each school acting as both prosecution and defence, in a challenging and realistic case in front of a packed court audience.

Cliff Slade, JP, who along with Sarah Gainer and Deputy Head Mr George House, helped the students to prepare for the case, and were delighted with the overall performance on the day. Mr Slade said directing a case from both defence and prosecution perspectives is a complicated, challenging and complex occasion for even a well-seasoned solicitor. Tenbury High School students directed both courts in a confident and professional manner and represented Tenbury School and themselves in a most commendable way. There were definitely a few budding 'legal eagles' in our midst. Although the competition was eventually won by St Augustine's School from Redditch, Tenbury will take great pride in their accomplishment and performance.

In 2009, I really was at the peak of my personal confidence in relationships, business activities and extracurricular activities. I really was peaking in my own self-actualisation. I really was truly myself and felt I had achieved and reached my full potential through creativity and independence. I was now looking for that ever-changing challenge and new direction that drives me forward. I love the Japanese word 'kaizen' – continuous improvement, and constantly believe in its definition and that I need constant personal development!

I decided to enter the world of politics and my first attempt was to jump in at County Councillor level, one level below an MP! Big ask, big challenge and big job! I have never lost. I couldn't lose. I have a vision and can see myself at the winning line. That belief is so powerful, and it works. I would need a clever pen, broad shoulders and the ability to answer a question without answering the question. I had to have a plan. No one really knew who or what I was outside of my personal friends and family. I needed to raise my profile without my local media knowing what I was up to and, in particular my election candidate rivals! I had a plan. No one told me or advised me; again I knew instinctively what I had to do. I always did!

I have never been interested in politics although I have never wasted my vote. My first vote, at the age of nineteen was in 1979 and I helped bring to power, Maggie Thatcher. With Margaret Thatcher in power for the next eleven years I, personally, grew in confidence, wealth and belief, although these days proved to be difficult times for the country as some industries and their workers such as the miners, the car industry and trade unions were suffering and experiencing misery and anguish well into the eighties and beyond. Eventually, the economy boomed, as did my creativity and drive, and I would forever be a conservative, for the time being. 1979 was also the year I noticed and attracted a human pure-bred, filly, race horse!

I honestly believed Tenbury at this time was unrepresented and needed a local individual to stand up and represent our community and its issues. Our sitting, Conservative councillor was retiring and had, for the past years of his last term in office, I felt, not really been active or interested – he was in his seventies! The Conservative party had already selected his predecessor, a certain Dr Ken Pollock, who was rumoured to live outside the boundary but was holding an address in the boundary for election purposes. This enraged not only my integrity DNA, but also my fairness and honesty sprit level. It was game on. I couldn't fail. I never have!

I had my plan and it was now time to initiate it! My first task was to raise my profile. I really did invent 'fake news' and my ability to write would take on a new level! Again, writing a letter is a little story. I just changed from calling my letter a letter, to calling it an article.

I invented stories, obviously with honesty and integrity, that got my name in the local media and got me noticed. I was going to raise my profile. I needed to get my name and picture in the media for good causes or no causes. My end agenda was to win an election.

The election was in May 2009, so I started my media elevation of myself early in December 2008 with a 'down memory lane' input. I sent in two photographs of two football teams I coached at Tenbury Primary school when all the children were around six or seven years old. They would now be around twenty years old – VOTING AGE! I wrote the story and sent it in with the photographs and hey presto, they printed it and it had the right effect. It brought memories back to all those kids who were now adults and they reminisced our good times together = twenty four votes. My name was also splattered a couple of times in the story for those readers who didn't know me – product placement!

Every Saturday morning at Tenbury Primary School this group of budding young foot-ballers met under the coaching of Mick King and Cliff Slade. The year was 1995 and all these lads were between six and eight. Today they will now be either out working or gaining their A level results and maybe going off to university. Sadly, none of them are gracing the likes of Old Trafford, but a few are still playing lo-cally on the hallowed turf of the Palmer's Meadow with the senior Tenbury United team.

The following week I released a story and forwarded to the press with me presenting a cheque in my position as Tenbury Town Band President!

Tenbury Town band members and associated family members = #? votes, plus my name and picture just to introduce myself and for people to get to know me; it was working!

CLIFF SLADE, PRESIDENT OF TENBURY TOWN BAND PRESENTS A CHEQUE TO IAN BALDRY

Tenbury Town Band's fund-raising efforts have been recognised by Help for Heroes county co-ordinator Ian Baldry.

Ian, a serving officer in the Territorial Army, paid tribute to Tenbury Town Band's tremendous effort in raising a substantial amount of money as Cliff Slade, band president, presented an £800 cheque.

Help for Heroes is a charity set up in 2007 to help armed forces personnel who have been seriously injured during operational duty. To date, it has raised more than £19 million.

A number of soldiers from the county's local regiment, the 2nd Battalion Mercian Regiment (Worcester and Sherwood Foresters), have received treatment at Headley Court following their last operational tour in Afghanistan. Headley Court is the Joint Services Rehabilitation Centre.

Mr Baldry presented the band with a certificate to recognise its achievement and every member also received a Help for Heroes wristband. The money was raised at a Christmas concert at The Regal and at a bingo session at the Regal Community Centre.

The following week, I released a story and picture of me becoming a Director of Worcester City Football Club. Two senior football teams and many football supporters in Tenbury, and me now watching Tenbury United play locally = a lot of votes!

The following week, I released a story of me at Tenbury High School in my capacity as magistrate mentoring the school's students who had entered the national schools' Mock Trials Competition! Twenty students and families, as well as potentially, the whole local school parent support = lots and lots of votes!

I was on a roll! People were now beginning to talk and remark, 'you are in the paper every week for something', 'am I?' This was good softening up and I hadn't even said a political sentence yet! Editors and journalists were eager for a story. This was a time of change within the media industry as digital media was causing cut backs and redundancies. A free story and picture were welcome for the hard-pressed journalists, so I took advantage and swamped the news desk with readymade articles and pictures. My stories were being printed word for word and what painted a thousand words was a good picture! I always sent a picture with my story taken by a local retired, successful press photographer, Jeremy Pardoe – a true professional in his trade. The best! Everything I sent in was going to press, not only locally, but also countywide! Pictures = votes!

Whenever something was on, in and around Tenbury, I was there, and I had a view or comment to make ready to be picked up by my local press! I attended a charity fundraising event and out-bid everyone on a *Mamma Mia* film poster, much to the extreme disappointment of a lady who was desperate for it. I paid for the poster then handed it over to the lady who really wanted it; she was overjoyed and promptly made a further donation to the cause. I was a hero and the local attending press guy wanted my photo - front page coverage = how many votes? Priceless poster?

POSTER SALE RAISES £260

It was smiles all round at the Community Centre in Tenbury Wells on Saturday, January 17, as a sale of film posters raised over £260. The proceeds will go towards making sure that film shows continue at The Regal. Dozens of people came to what proved to be an enjoyable and memorable morning, with many of us taking home a memento of a Regal film show.

There were plenty of posters to choose from, ranging from *Mamma Mia*, *James Bond* and *Harry Potter*, to a host of less prominent films. The posters came from two

sources, some from the volunteer group
that now shows films at The Regal, others
were donated by the Wall family, who kept
the films running for many years. Without
them, Tenbury might have lost its cinema
some time ago, as happened in most small
market towns.

These days, the film shows are run by
a team of volunteers, headed by Ben
Bydawell. He said, 'I'm really pleased
that so many people came,' while David
Hambelton, a stalwart of the Regal Cinema
Volunteer Group, commented on how well the
morning had gone.
Top bid was £60 for a *Mamma Mia* poster,
which sold to local businessman Cliff
Slade, who promptly donated the poster
back, so that it could be resold to raise
further funds.

Cliff explained, 'I heard about the
meeting and decided to pop in and buy a
few posters, as this was a good opportunity to make a donation and have a cup of
tea, while supporting The Regal. In the
past, I spent many happy hours there
watching films with my children. Some
posters were displayed on the walls and
one for *Mamma Mia* caught my eye. I finally
became the winning bidder, but I was aware
that the other bidder was a serious *Mamma
Mia* enthusiast and could sense her disappointment. My only reason for attending

was to make a donation and support the voluntary body that runs The Regal, so I immediately informed this lady that she was welcome to the poster and gave my reasons for bidding for it. She was very pleased to be the new owner. The lady did also make a generous donation and the overall winners were The Regal Supporters'.

There were many other stories I invented and comments I made on nonsense issues such as a heavy goods vehicle damaging 'the round historical market' in Tenbury Wells. My name and photo were everywhere. I penned this next letter, which was the last non-political one, before I started to turn into a political activist and an election candidate. My writing style was about to change, and I was about to fire the starting pistol!

Dear Editor,
    May I through your column express my thanks and appreciation for a recent event I had the pleasure to attend?
    On the evening of Saturday the fourteenth of December 2008, I sacrificed the televised 'X Factor' and 'Strictly Come Dancing' final to attend the Tenbury Town Band Christmas Concert. The whole evening was a most enjoyable occasion which far exceeded my expectations. Not only was the

band splattered with the usual youngsters
and senior members, but the sound and rep-
ertoire for the evening was truly rousing.

TTB were supported by The Waterloo
Band & Bugles, The Rifles Band, and the
choir of St Lawrence Primary School, Ludlow. This, coupled with festive solo singing from semi-professional vocalist, Lynne
Hawkins, and various other solo pieces
from members of the band, sent the packed
house home full of mulled wine, mince pies
and a real sense of Christmas cheer. Thank
you, Tenbury Town Band for a great Christmas variety night, and all in the aid of
the charity 'Help the Heroes'.

Cliff Slade

At this point it was always in my mind to stand as an
independent candidate. I would then be in charge of myself, what I had to say, and how I was going to represent
the West Worcestershire Division!

This was my first letter to be printed with a political
view, albeit, it was subtle and still guarded, but it was a
change of direction.

Dear Editor,
As per Joe Roseman's letter, (Advertiser 11th December 2008.) I also received
the recent campaign leaflet from Richard

Burt, the Liberal Democratic prospective candidate, for the next general election.

Contrary to Joe Roseman's view, I feel this is what 'politics is all about'. Surely, we could do a lot worse than elect Richard Burt, who would make just the sort of MP we are looking for. Has he not got a duty and responsibility to identify, and bring to the attention shortcomings in past, present and future governments and their representatives? As it's the appropriate season, perhaps we could take Richard Burt's leaflet as 'a kinda Christmas Carol' message in politics to us all! As we all know, the leading character 'saw the light' and changed his views, beliefs, and values by facing the ghosts in all eras.

Rather than be in denial, may I, respectively, suggest that Joe Roseman reviews and applies Dickens' social writing and philosophies. We need to consider others' vision, analyses and views!

We need alternatives, we need new strategies, we need new leaders, or we are destined for more and protracted 'hard times'!

More please, Richard Burt!

Merry Christmas,

Cliff Slade

Richard Burt was the Liberal Democratic parliamentary candidate, and this election was to take place shortly after my county council election. The Liberals were strong contenders for the 2010 election, and the party to lose out was forecasted to be the Labour party! Although this letter and the following letters were now political and had a political agenda, they were still my personal and genuine comments and views. I believe that if I am genuine, grateful and honest, I can't fail, as this was my authentic character. Again, some humour and tongue-in-cheek remarks were endearing and moreish to the reader, but unbeknown to them, they were now my target electorate!

At this point, the Liberals and local Liberal activists considered the West Worcestershire parliamentary seat as a key seat. If they had a strong candidate at county council level, and put some resources into this election, they could win. I was approached by them, with a view to standing as a Liberal Democrat candidate for the county council seat. If I could win this seat before the general election, it would put Richard Burt in a stronger position and I became a target, a potential candidate for them, so they sent a representative around to court me. Councillor George Price, former mayor, leader of Malvern Hills District, past County Councillor candidate and a hardened anti-Tory activist, was sent to meet me.

In the meantime, another letter, a political letter. It's now time to ratchet up the ante. I still believe what I was writing about was an injustice and unfair, but this was now fuelling my potential political ambition, as well as tapping into my integrity and fairness DNA.

TEMESIDE HOUSE PLEDGE BROKEN?

I have a 'new year' conundrum for the people of Tenbury to consider! In an article within the Tenbury Advertiser (24/12/08), Cllr Phil Grove informs us the District Council has 'given' the 'pump rooms' to Tenbury Town Council, and they will soon be moving their offices into this fine Victorian former salt baths.

When this handing over ceremony finally takes place, (no doubt with a photo of Cllr Grove proudly handing over the keys) will the keys also be accompanied with a pledge from the District Council to continue Tenbury rate-payers' current 'Temeside council office' payment terms, i.e. nominal rent, nominal rates and maintenance etc? Or are Tenbury Town Council accepting full responsibility for maintenance? And what about if something minor, moderate or even catastrophic happens to this fine old building? WHO PAYS? Not sure about you, but I'm starting to think Tenbury Town Council may be forced to set a new local tax levy to accommodate these potentially costly 'what ifs' for our 'gift'. If this is the case, what have we, the people of Tenbury, actually been given? I've got it! NOTHING! Sorry, yes we have. MORE MONEY to pay in our rates next year and subsequent years to come!

Hang on a minute! The people of Tenbury voted Cllr Grove onto the District Council with a pledge, promise, statement and assurance, that in the event of Temeside Council Offices being sold off, the proceeds would go directly to the town of Tenbury. Is Cllr Grove reneging on his pledge or was this just a political promise 'at the time'? As he now informs us, the proceeds will be spent and swallowed up on 'projects' all over the district.

Have our conservative-led district councillors only 'sold us down the river'? Has our local council been hoodwinked and more importantly, who's paying for our gift?

Happy New Year!

Cliff Slade

I was whisked away to Worcestershire County Hall and introduced to, interviewed and courted by the sitting Liberal Democratic councillors and their officials. After much deliberation, I decided to join the party and was announced as their County Council candidate for the forthcoming May 2009 elections. My decision was based on the fact I could influence any decisions for my area as part of a party and group of people rather than as an independent individual! At my request, it was also agreed that the Liberal Democratic logo would be used only, and not the full Liberal Democratic Party name. I wanted a low-profile association with the Lib Dems as my name was already respected and known, and my community CV was politically strong. They were pleased; so was I, albeit my conservative roots, values and beliefs were now compromised!

My candidature was announced in various local media outlets.

LIB DEMS PICK THEIR MAN FOR ELECTION

Businessman and JP, Cliff Slade, has been selected as the Liberal Democrat candidate for Tenbury Division in the county council elections in June.

Mr Slade will contest the seat following the retirement of long-serving county councillor, Reg Farmer, who will step down at the end of this term.

Mr Slade has lived in Tenbury Wells since 1975 and is managing director of a UK wide transport training business with offices in the centre of the town.

He is married to Julie, a former Tenbury Carnival Queen and they have two grown-up children.

He served as a Special Constable for five years and as a retained firefighter in Tenbury for 11 years.

'I'm very much looking forward to the challenges ahead and I put myself forward as I feel very strongly about Tenbury and surrounding villages being neglected and want to champion local issues where it matters at county level,' said Mr Slade.

He is a former Tenbury High School pupil and the president of Tenbury Town Band. He is also director of Worcester City Football Club.

I needed some upstanding members of my local community to sign and propose me as a candidate. Those people again, I am eternally grateful to. They put their head above the parapet and endorsed me for no gain for themselves, just nice, genuine people supporting me for nothing: George Price, Alan Dale and Cecil Everall - all well-known, popular individuals in their own right. Cecil, many years later, sadly passed away at the fantastic age of 92. Immediately, I penned a hand-written note to his wife. It's easy to write when it's genuine and from the heart!

Dear Jean,

So sorry to learn about Cec. It is so sad, and I really am sad and feel for you at this time. I enjoyed randomly but regularly meeting Cec to and fro from the shop as he took his regular constitution down town. Despite his aging frame, his mind, body and spirit were very much alive and so sharp. His wit, humour and ability to laugh never left him and we would always, without fail, part each other with that great smile of his.

A few years ago, I needed someone who was respected in the community to endorse and sign my electoral nomination papers. This information is then made public. Despite Cec's political and social standing he endorsed me and my nomination documents and for this I was so grateful and proud to have his name on those papers. It takes a special person to step forward and support someone in the way he did. Cec was a special, intelligent, genuine, lovely gentleman and greatly respected, particularly by me.

Cec was clearly devoted to you and adored you and would regularly include you in our conversation. He also glowed with pride whenever he talked about his children and grandchildren, and his family clearly meant so much to him.

Jean, I am thinking about you and please knock the door if you need anything or even a cuppa at any time.

Cliff

It was now time to write, attract, politicise, debate and get myself in and amongst the people and get people talking about me and making myself known to the opposition. I needed to get the opposition defending themselves against what I was saying; I would then be getting double exposure! I love the Oscar Wilde quote: 'there is only one thing in Tenbury worse than being talked about, and that is not being talked about'. I can't believe he said Tenbury!

I needed a hook; as in my business success I needed something different. I needed something to present the same but different. I needed to represent something that meant something to most people, something that was topical, and something to get my photo and my name in newspapers – POTHOLES!

This appeared on the front page of every local newspaper; it certainly struck a chord with the editors. I always sent in a picture with my story. I always used Jeremy

Pardoe as his pictures were different. I always controlled and suggested to Jeremy what I wanted, and the picture painted a thousand words. I gave the editor a packaged report so they didn't have to do anything with my piece apart from send it to the printers. I would be a complete news provider, so my stories and pictures were always printed word for word, and my letter writing skills were now mini media stories. Editors and journalists were under pressure, very busy and would grab anything I sent to them as they didn't have to do anything with the piece. They even put their name to my story. I didn't care whose name was on the report as long as it was my name being headlined!

WE GET A RAW DEAL WHEN IT COMES TO ROAD REPAIR

A Tenbury businessman is warning that roads in the town and surrounding area are dangerous because they are not being repaired.

Cliff Slade believes that rural parts of Worcestershire such as Tenbury are getting a raw deal when it comes to road repairs.

'There is a real safety issue, never mind the cost of the damage being caused to cars and other vehicles', said Mr Slade, who runs the Transport Training

Agency in Teme Street and has been a businessman in the town for nine years.

'Potholes are left and some of these are huge. A vehicle that hits one of these could easily be thrown into pedestrians on the pavement.

'At a time when money is tight, the cost of damage to tyres and suspension is a real issue for people who are struggling to make ends meet.

'On many roads and pathways we find ourselves negotiating potholes, uneven areas and broken surfaces in an attempt not only to preserve our own safety and the safety of others, but also to avoid potentially costly repairs to our vehicles.'

He says rural areas such as Tenbury are getting a particularly raw deal from Worcestershire County Council.

'It is a fact that an additional £15 million has been spend on roads in urban areas of the county but the rural network is now dangerously neglected and in a dreadful state of repair', said Mr Slade.

'This, coupled with worsening weather conditions, is now seriously compounding this potentially disastrous problem for drivers and pedestrians alike.'

Mr Slade, who will be a candidate in the county council elections later this year, thinks that transport chiefs fail to understand the importance of roads to people living in isolated rural communities.

'More rural families rely on these roads for daily essential journeys so why should we be placed in a situation where we are expected to commute on less safe roads because of our postcode?

'It is not unusual for roads to be in a poor condition at this time of the year, but things seem to be getting worse.'

This front-page article really pressed a lot of buttons; the response was incredible from the opposition, supporters and sitting councillors. A flurry of letters and features followed, and I was centre of attention. My name was everywhere, and the picture was being reused with other people's comments in support or attacking me! This was the sitting councillor's letter response to me – bingo!

TOWN HAS NOT HAD A RAW ROADS' DEAL
I am the county councillor for Tenbury and have been so for the past twelve years.

On the front page of the Advertiser on Thursday, February 19, you published statements made by Cliff Slade that Tenbury town and surrounding area is getting a raw deal when it comes to road repairs.

He is completely mistaken about that. County councils throughout the country have had to deal with severe weather conditions stretching their resources to the limit.

This has come at a time when councils are facing very difficult financial problems. It is easy to be negative, much more difficult to suggest the best way of solving problems that do not involve spending increased amounts of tax payers' money.

I can assure the people of Tenbury and the surrounding area that the damage caused to our roads by the severe weather will be repaired as soon as possible. The streets and pavements of Tenbury are without question the best maintained in the country by a very dedicated council employee.

For a number of years I have been encouraging local parish councils to employ a lengthsman. In the parishes who have engaged lengthsmen, highways are better maintained.

Coun Reg Farmer

I quickly responded and letters after letters after letters after letters rolled in! I always included both naturally and purposely, humour content; this knack seemed to be attractive, engaging and endearing. People were stopping me and telling me my letters were very funny whilst still making a point, and they always looked for my name. If my name wasn't there, they didn't bother to read the other letters! I poured on the momentum. 'The letters' forum was being bombarded with me!

POTHOLES ARE NOT JUST WINTER WEAR
In response to County Councillor Reg Farmer's letter (Advertiser, March 6) claiming Tenbury and surrounding district roads and pathways are not in a poor state, this is just beyond belief.

Perhaps we are all wrong, or is Coun Farmer wearing the Emperor's new suit?

These potholes are certainly not just winter weather wear. Margaret Austin has been campaigning for five years in some cases.

Is it a coincidence or am I being cynical, but did my recent campaign, both directly to the county council and via the Advertiser regarding the unacceptable conditions of Tenbury and district roads and pathways, prompt a visit to Tenbury Town Council last week of John Wallace, county highways liaison engineer?

Is it also a coincidence that the previous week Tenbury and surrounding district experienced a mini phenomenon in the form of a road repair team?

John Wallace informed the town council meeting that the deep pothole, splash point and noise pollution the Kyrewood

Road potholes were causing have been classified as 'not a priority'. He also informs us there is now insufficient funding available.

Here is something positive and constructive for Coun Farmer to consider. Is it more financially viable to spend our tax on having seven road teams a year running around the county doing temporary jobs every time we have a downpour? Would not some preventative maintenance be in order and being proactive in the summer rather than reactive in the winter be more constructive and economical?

I remember what now seems a faint past memory while walking past a road repair team cringing at the deafening hammering of the pneumatic drill and a mini earthquake as the heavy vibrating roller sealed the pothole for good.

My old woodwork teacher used to smack me around the head and say, 'measure twice and cut once'.

CLIFF SLADE

Councillor Farmer responded – the media even re-published my photo – free publicity! Everything was going to plan!

PUBLIC MONEY IS NOT LIMITLESS

In the letter published on March 12, Cliff Slade shows he has no understanding of how local authorities work.

The maintenance of highways is one of the many responsibilities county councils

have, using government funding (taxpayers' money) and ratepayers' money. They have to work to a yearly budget.

As reported in the Advertiser, John Wallace, head of Worcestershire County Council's highways department, told Tenbury Town Council that potholes happen every year all over the county, especially after a winter where there has been a lot of rain and snow – 'where a pothole was dangerous, they were dealt with quickly'.

However, there

are other factors affecting our local roads – the government allowed the weight of lorries to increase to 46 tonnes, farming practises have changed. In the Tenbury area, we now have a large potato growing industry, which has my support; however it necessitates the use of large heavy tractors and trailers. Over a period of several weeks they make numerous journeys to local storage warehouses along small country roads and around Tenbury town.

There is always a limit to the amount of public money available. Councils have to ensure it is spent wisely.

Coun Reg Farmer
Worcestershire County Council
representative for Tenbury

I responded again with humour, and the media played my game with a further photograph, again carefully orchestrated by me!

DICTIONARY DEFINITIONS CAN COME IN HANDY

In response to Coun Reg Farmer's letter
(Advertise, March 26) suggesting I have no
understanding of how local authorities
work, to the contrary, I understand how
they don't work.

I went to Tenbury High School some
time ago now. In my early years I was
taught to use a dictionary. I still use
these skills now - I looked up the definition of councillor. It states: 'Member of

local government elected to run the administrative affairs of a local district'.

The affairs of our local district, particularly the roads, are in a dreadful state. During my campaign through the Advertiser, I have received a mass of letters demanding we have our share of the money we contribute via our taxes and rates spent on our roads.

I have had angry telephone calls from residents and farmers in Rochford, Handley Childe, Bockleton, Clifton, Abberley and Stoke Bliss to mention just a few, demanding these long overdue repairs are actioned.

One other key element within the definition of councillor is 'elected'.

Councillor Farmer's final long paragraph within his letter relates to potatoes – what on earth have potatoes got to do with potholes?

However, just to demonstrate my dexterity with my dictionary, 'potatoes are a perennial plant grown for human consumption and they are also used in the manufacture of alcohol and adhesives'. Similarly, potatoes are perennial and perhaps we could use their adhesive qualities and throw some into the potholes to seal them.

We want our money invested in Tenbury and districts, not excuses. Looks as though Tenbury has missed out again. One

thing that can be said about me is that I
am quick.

I was from a large family and things
were hard then as well. When we got up in
the morning, first down the stairs was the
best dressed.

Cliff Slade

I had literally started a pothole war and invented
myself as the self-styled Pothole King of South Worcestershire. The stories and letters went on and on and on and
would form a standalone book in themselves! I was also
proving the confidence in myself was powerful and my
energy and ambition was driven by the belief I could do
anything, be anything, win anything, succeed in anything
and think differently because I was different, because
nothing got in my way, because I didn't have any barriers,
because barriers are only built by ourselves and my foundations of my childhood had no critical obstructions! I
didn't have a plan on how I was going to win; you don't
have to have it all worked out to move forward. I never
did. I was living in the now and what was happening
now, and that is how I was going to move forward and
win against all the odds! But for now, more potholes!

POTHOLE WARS
Local people have responded with derision
to the claims that their Conservative
county councillor in a recent letter to

the press, said Tenbury district's roads are better than they have ever been!

Cliff has offered to give the Leader of the County Council a tour round the villages to show him the problems, since he said Tenbury 'wasn't his patch'! Cliff will continue to press for extra money to repair rural roads, pavements and foot-paths.

Once again, you have told me in your responses to my survey how strongly you feel about the state of our roads. On your behalf, I took my campaign to the media and to the Leader of the County Council. This resulted in a visit to Tenbury from a highways officer responsible and a road repair team visiting Tenbury to fill in a few potholes. But still this is JUST NOT GOOD ENOUGH!

Angry Potholers at Hanley Childe

Cliff met with frustrated residents of Hanley Childe with huge potholes at Hanley Childe.

Just another example of OUR AREA missing out!

Cliff Slade

I wrote letters and passed them to my friends suggesting and inviting them to post them to our local media and they did.

TENBURY NEEDS A TRUE LOCAL VOICE
Now that Cliff Slade has thrown himself forward for the county elections, we should have a really interesting contest.

Whoever wins, what Tenbury really needs is a true local voice who will speak up for the people of the town.

That is why I cannot understand why the Conservatives have selected a candidate from down the Teme valley, while Phil Grove is fighting a seat in Malvern, twenty three miles away.

He cannot be spending much time looking after Tenbury if he is knocking on the doors of West Malvern.

I think the Conservatives may have shot themselves in both feet on this occasion!

A.N. Other
Tenbury Wells
(AKA Cliff Slade!)

CANDIDATES THROW HATS INTO RING

Dear Editor,

Having read through the Tenbury Advertiser in recent weeks, I notice that we now have two candidates who have thrown their hats in the ring to represent Tenbury Wells at County Council level.

Mr Ken Pollock the latest candidate, claims to have lived in Tenbury for thirty years, which was a major surprise to me as I have never seen or heard of him before and I have lived here all my life, perhaps one of your readers could shed some light on this obvious oversight or was this a slip of his pen!

To this end, I noticed in some recent literature through my post box from a Mr Ken Pollock of Great Whitley. Could this be the same person or am I confused!

Will the real Ken Pollock please 'stand up'?

I am aware of the other candidate who I do know lives in Tenbury Wells. Mr Cliff Slade, whom not only has lived in the area for a considerable time but is also a valuable employer.

As it was stated a few weeks back in the Advertiser, we need to attract new businesses and support the existing employers of Tenbury Wells, the growing trend in unemployment is a major concern for many people. The likes of Mr Slade would be an invaluable asset representing us on the County Council, having successfully built two businesses and employing people from Tenbury Wells.

Regards,

A.N. Other
(AKA Cliff Slade!)

I started getting up the noses of the senior county hall and district councillors and got a response from the leader and wrote to him via the letters page!

TENBURY ON THE A456 IN WEST WORCESTERSHIRE
I would like to personally invite the
leader of Worcestershire County Council,
Councillor George Lord, to Tenbury Wells.
In a recent letter I wrote to him regard-
ing the appalling state of our roads in
and around Tenbury Wells and he commented
'Tenbury is not on my patch'.

My letter was then passed onto Councillor, Derek Prodger, who has responsibility for environment at County Hall and
he seems to think our roads in and around
Tenbury Wells are safer now than they were
five years ago.

Cllr Prodger in his correspondence also informs me any road damage or defects
identified are actioned quickly and efficiently. Town Councillor Margaret Austin
has been campaigning for five years for a
particular defect to be actioned – hardly
'quick action'! The serious pothole I
identified was repaired in days. That same
pothole some days later was showing signs
of deterioration – hardly 'efficient'!

This is not just adverse weather deterioration or a cold weather snap! Perhaps
a little preventative maintenance prior to
winter would have minimised the appalling
situation Tenbury and surrounding district
roads are currently in!

For Cllr Lord's information Tenbury is
about twenty miles South West of Worcester

on the A456. I am prepared to pick both of them up at County Hall and take our distinguished guests on a tour of our local roads around Clifton on Teme, Rochford, Lindridge, Eastham and Abberley and they can then have the opportunity to affirm our road surfaces and conditions are safe!

I read with interest more 'road repairing' teams (seven) are being despatched from the County Council as 'improving footpath and highway services is a county council priority, and that means keeping the roads maintained to a high standard'.

Perhaps while I am at County Hall picking up my guests one of the repair teams could follow me over to Tenbury!

Cliff Slade

IS OUR LOCAL CONSERVATIVE COUNCILLOR DESERTING US?

Cllr Phil Grove has introduced himself to the electorate in Trinity Division in Malvern as their local County Council Candidate and their 'local champion'! (He lives in Tenbury!)

What happened to being a local champion for Tenbury?

Is this why Tenbury is not being represented? Is this why Tenbury is so neglected? Is this why Tenbury has not got a voice?

While our local champion has taken his eye of the ball and is concentrating on carpet bagging Trinity Division in Malvern, we hear Malvern Hills District Council are funding £140k annually of our tax money on Malvern Theatre. Yet the volunteer group running The Regal Cinema in Tenbury receives nothing. Whilst Cllr Grove has been planning his campaign in Malvern how much progress on developing Tenbury Business Park has been made during his time in office? Whilst Cllr Grove introduces himself to Malvern, maybe we could reflect on his recent efforts to stimulate Tenbury's local economy after the floods!

Has Cllr Grove just used Tenbury as a 'stepping stone' for his own personal political ambitions?

The next thing the Conservatives will be informing us is that we have a new Conservative representative in Tenbury who does not live in our area!

Bon voyage, Cllr Grove, although I wonder if the people of Malvern will be gullible enough to accept you as their local champion. We, in Tenbury, will look after ourselves. Looks as if we will have to!

I wonder if his decision to jump ship will not, in the words of that well-known

poem, become a 'stumbling block' rather
than a 'stepping stone?'

Cliff Slade

Momentum was now on a roll, but I needed more than potholes. I looked for every opportunity to engage and generate publicity. I was talking dog poo, brick walls crumbling, floods, wheelie bins, speeding, fire cuts – crikey! I needed pictures, pictures, pictures which always succeeded for the over-worked journalists and editors. I was saving them a lot of work; I was a mini whirlwind newspaper journalist. I bombarded them with articles and they always printed them every week. Although I was creating news and looking for opportunities, I was still genuine, I was still authentic and wanted to make a difference for people and champion their particular cause or concern. That is what people recognise and attract; attraction is being genuine. Respecting justice and integrity really are in my DNA and matter to me.

Pothole rest – I moved onto some local speed issues!

Cliff Slade is to initiate a petition to send to County Hall demanding more to be done in light of yet another example of Tenbury resident concerns being lost in the abyss. Oldwood resident, Sandra Gill, has had a vehicle collide with her house as a result of a speeding car along Oldwood Road.

Roy Coley and Doreen Coley, along with many more residents in Redgate Avenue,

have had many near misses whilst exiting Redgate Avenue due to speeding cars on the Oldwood Road. Mr Coley said he has written many times to the Highways Department at County Hall highlighting his concerns. He said, 'this is a serious accident waiting to happen'.

Cliff Slade with his petition with Redgate residents, Roy Coley, Doreen Coley, and Oldwood resident, Sandra Gill.

Flood defence for Tenbury:

'WE MUST NOT GIVE UP ON FLOOD DEFENCES'

Cliff Slade has written to Environment Agency Flood Protection Manager, Anthony Perry, to find out what people in Tenbury need to do to get flood defences for the town. Cliff attended a recent public meeting on flooding, and was disappointed by the lack of progress towards getting defences. Now, he has responded to the challenge made by Mr Perry in a recent newspaper article calling for Tenbury to find a way forward. 'Anthony Perry said that there were a number of possibilities that people in the town council could pursue, and I want to find out from him what he has in mind', said Cliff. 'It is vital that Tenbury gets its flood defences for residents and businesses in the town to face the future with any kind of confidence.'

Cliff down by the calm river which must be tamed for good!

Engage with the people and listen but more importantly get a picture of me gesturing, looking as if I know what I'm talking about, Messiah look!

Fire cuts with Richard Burt, the parliamentary candidate...anything!

Wheelie bins – wheelie!

Crumbling brick walls – note the face. Note my reassuring hand on the nearly victim's shoulder. I'm nearly giggling, you cannot be serious! This was making front page news. I was bricking it.

Liberal Democrat parliamentary candidate, Richard Burt, joined local businessman and County Council candidate, Cliff Slade on his latest 'walk for business' in Tenbury town centre last week.

I was into everything, but it was now the time of reckoning! – I had turned the town orange – polling day!

Everyone wished me 'good luck' and local business owners supported me.

The conservatives, particularly in a rural location like West Worcestershire, turn out in their droves at election time; they are tribal and their voting colour is generational. They always turn out and vote. Even if they put a blue rosette on a mutt they will vote for it! I could just nick this win if I could attract the socialist vote and the individuals who were in the pub and probably had never bothered to vote! This, coupled with the liberal support, and the fact I was popular and known in my community, meant it was going to be close.

Thursday, the fourth of June 2009 and after six months of clever campaigning, people in Tenbury were turning out in one of the highest recorded turn outs in the area's voting past. I was outside the polling station in Tenbury and the feeling was positive – I could do this! I went to my office with Julie and got on the phone with my business office staff. I drummed those people who would probably not bother to vote and we called them. I needed their vote; it was going to be close.

All my writing skills, all my relationships, talking, embracing, charisma, humour, charm, personality and allure were all put to use, and the next day at Worcester we attended the count. All the returns were in and my main opponent was hovering over the ballot papers, and my piles and his piles were neck and neck throughout the count. I was excited; he was troubled and nervous. In the last election, the conservatives had had a majority win of over three thousand. This was certainly not going to be the same. I suddenly thought whether I had to stand on the stage in line with the other candidates as the returning officer announces the result for South Worcestershire and then make my victorious speech. I took George, my political mentor, to one side and questioned him on the etiquette at the result ceremony and asked whether I was expected to say anything. Apparently, I had been watching too much parliamentary election television and he informed me that the result would be announced, and I would not have to say anything apart from congratulate, commiserate and shake hands with my attending opponents on a closely fought campaign! George said, 'you have got this, you are going to win!' You really could not tell the result. The piles of ballot papers and the anticipation were growing. Heads were shaking and nodding and my opponent was like a hawk watching the counting team and checking they were doing their job correctly.

I took time out in a side room with Julie and a few others, and that is when George and Richard and other members of the election team came in and informed me that I had narrowly missed out by a few hundred votes, and a recount was considered but decided against. My opponents came in, shook my hand and congratulated me on a well-fought campaign, as did Reg Farmer, the former conservative councillor of this seat, and he said, 'what happened to my three and a half thousand majority?'

Over the following few days, I reflected on my losing, and I was genuinely disappointed for Julie and the team around me and everything they did to support, help and guide me, but more importantly, I was disappointed for the individuals who put a tick against my name who trusted and believed in me. I was humbly grateful.

What did I do? I wrote a letter!

GREAT EXPERIENCE ON ELECTION TRAIL

Through your columns, may I take the opportunity to thank the residents and businesses of Tenbury Wells and surrounding villages for the tremendous support I received during the County Council elections.

Although I was unsuccessful in my bid to represent Tenbury division, I was so very humbled by the support, help, best wishes and encouragement I received throughout my campaign.

This was my very first effort, and the only occasion I have put myself forward to the electorate of Tenbury.

I am, of course, very disappointed that I did not succeed in my quest, as I can truly say I have the best interests of our area at heart.

My only motivation was to action so many people's unheard issues and concerns in this beautiful area, and to represent the fantastic people I feel privileged to live with. However, I have been, and will continue to get involved in community projects and organisations, both now, and in the future.

Although there are too many individuals to thank, it evokes special feelings when someone puts a window sticker or a garden poster on their residence or business publicly supporting you.

Similarly, it is a brave individual or business person, who is prepared to supply a written endorsement, both publicly and privately, and it is also endearing when individuals volunteer to post, fetch, carry and call on your behalf.

It was so heartening to firstly speak to people on their doorsteps, and then meet them on polling day turning out to cast their vote, in particular, the elderly people, when at times every step they were taking was clearly a great effort.

Equally, it was also uplifting to see so many young people casting their very first vote with an exciting thumbs up.

The whole election process has been so very interesting, enjoyable and exciting; it has been a great opportunity to meet old acquaintances, colleagues and friends. Along the way, I have also met so many new friends and interesting people who I will be revisiting and maintaining contact with in the future.

For the record, and rounding up figures, I received 1,400 votes in second place versus the winning candidate's 1,700 votes. I was at the count, and up until the final moment, it was too close to call, which added to the excitement.

The turnout in Tenbury was some 49 per cent, which was phenomenal.

Eight out of ten people in Tenbury voted for me but, unfortunately, I lost ground in the rural areas.

I, of course, congratulate Ken Pollock on his success, and I wish him luck for his period representing us all at County Hall.

For my part, I am off to get my shoes resoled and rub more aftersun lotion on to my receding hair line, and just like in Arnie Schwarzenegger's famous movie, 'I'll be back!'

Once again, a very sincere thank you for all the cards and telephone calls, and to everyone who supported me. It was a great experience.

CLIFF SLADE

How did I personally feel and why did I lose? As mentioned earlier, I felt disappointed for other people rather than for me personally. Being grateful for other people's efforts on my behalf, as I said in the thank you letter, is very special and humbling. My immediate family, of course, would have liked me to win. My character is really not competitive, as in my childhood I had no one to really encourage, watch or shout me on in sporting competitions, matches, races or challenges. To come second and not be noticed was OK but that does mean I always do my best for me, not anyone else. If ever I thought, 'surely, I couldn't do that', I had to put myself up for it. I had to do it, no matter how challenging, how painful, how scary, how impossible, and how fearful that particular thought was. I had to do it, and this was the case as a County Council candidate. I didn't win but I had won. I was the best candidate anyone could have been and personally, I had again grown, learnt and developed. I was the biggest winner and I felt great. I had won. I had gained the most. I was a better person throughout the whole experience. I had exorcised and faced my personal fears and inhibitions. I had again felt the fear and done it anyway. I was on a high from my achievement of having taken part and putting myself forward.

Everything I do, be it win, lose or take part, I have always had a vision, always believed, always known, imagined and saw myself achieving and being successful – so why didn't I win? Because I had a doubt as to my political persuasion. Because at the age of nineteen years old, I cast my very first vote and brought into power Margaret Thatcher, and the subsequent years were very successful for me. There was a little doubt, and that little doubt prevented me winning that election!

For now, that was the end of my political ambitions, and this is the end of my observations and writing of letters at this time. I opened this election trail chapter with the paragraph below.

'In 2009, I really was at the peak of my personal confidence in relationships, business activities and extracurricular activities. I was peaking in my own self-actualisation. I was truly myself, and I felt I had achieved and reached my full potential through creativity and independence.'

This point of 'self-actualisation' was reached with a lifetime of ever-changing, emotional enlightenments and physical and mental, painful challenges. Elements of my character were blocked and layered for emotional self-preservation and survival. Elements I feared conquering or confronting were deep-seated and put in place by my own conditioning shield. For me, the term 'self-actualisation' represents the fact that I had recognised my fears and weaknesses emotionally, spiritually, physically and mentally. I had recognised my conditions and challenged them with pain, anguish and by being fearless and taking risks - risks that, at times, are personal, emotional torture even today. Just one example from many is that today, in the event of my being required to stand up and speak, my stomach churns, my heart beats in my chest, my mouth dries up, and the pain and fear are almost unbearable. I still have that feeling that I had as that child in class being asked a question by the teacher. I just wanted to be the quiet, listening, invisible child in my inner sanctuary, where no one could reach me. But despite these feelings, I realised that my potential, ability, talent and possibilities were never going to be realised unless I felt the fear and did it anyway. With that pain and anguish pitted in the base of my stomach, I always rise to my feet and speak – self-actualisation'.

My journey of self-actualisation is a lifetime evolution that, for me, began in 1979. In the late spring of 1979, I was in a queue in my local newsagents waiting to buy a newspaper and twenty Embassy Regal. As I was being served at the counter, I was drawn to, and got fixated on, this incredibly slender waist, perfectly rounded bottom and the darkest, perfectly straight, long, black, shiny hair which almost reached down to this impeccably-formed bottom. This seemingly fantastical illusion was wearing a pair of spray on cream corduroy trousers with the longest pair of legs I had ever seen; these legs looked as if they belonged to a pure-bred race horse! It was my old mate, Steve, from the iron monger shop…sorry I'm being silly. This pedigree vision in front of me was obviously a top-class filly and, as she turned around to exit the shop, she faced me and the front visualisation just completely complemented the rear exterior. She was olive-skinned with deep brown eyes, jet black eyebrows that harmonised with her dark hair, high cheekbones with thick, fat, juicy lips, and she was wearing a deep purple top, unbuttoned at the top. The purple, royal colour gave her a regal look, and she exited with a bouncy model walk like a debutante with royal aloofness! If I were to write myself a letter of that experience, it would read:

```
Dear Cliff,
     Who the fok was that? Phew!
                              Cliff Slade
```

At this time, early 1979, life was good. I had my car, earned loads of money, had the top guy job of loading lorries on the forklift trucks, and I even played in a band. At weekends, I was at the local disco and kept practising drinking beer. I had had a few female experiences under my belt and had just cast my first vote that delivered Margaret Thatcher into office, and the whole country and world seemed to have an air of 'feel-good' including me.

As summer approached, working in a pop factory in the summer was a good place to be. It was busy, and overtime was plentiful, but more importantly, students would arrive temporarily to work in between college or university. Students, as in female students, came and we could show off racing around on our trucks and who knows, maybe attract one. We were all between seventeen and twenty three years old, the same as the students – the female students. We all waited with excitement for the rapid uplift in production, despatch and sales, so we could cast our young eyes over the new recruits, the new female recruits.

As they arrived, I could not believe the racing horse, pure-bred filly was clocking in. 'Who's that?' I said, 'keep your eyes off that,' Mick Marston, one of the lorry drivers said, 'she's too good for you, you've got no chance, she lives with me and she is a lesbian', he chuckled. I chased him around the yard and he ran like a little gingerbread man, laughing his head off. I was later to learn she was living with him as she was his wife's sister. She was single and had just split 'up-ish' with her boyfriend. Her name was Julie Sheldon.

My happy disposition, my constant positive outlook, the great defender of the good, and truth and fighter of negativity comes out in letters – I can't help it. At the start of a new year, January 2018, a front-page, pessimistic, anti-Brexit article appeared from a local business man. How depressing! This needs addressing and defending, and if I thought that, so did others. Time for a letter!

Dear Sir,

Every now and then I write a letter to the Tenbury Advertiser. On the whole, the feedback I get around the town seems to be that I generally write about what other people are feeling or thinking. Surely I am, therefore, not the only person who read the front page leading story (Advertiser, 11th January, 2018) from John Foster, and his 'fears' for 2018 as a rather dismal and gloomy outlook for the ensuing year! I then turned the pages and within his 'viewpoint', the whole sorry saga was repeated. How depressing! Mr Foster's views and comments are, of course, constructed around his strong anti-Brexit stance. Arguably, he may or may not be correct. For many reasons, I was also a 'remainer', but I whole-heartedly embrace the will of the democratic decision, and I am very much looking forward, and remain equally positive to the challenges we, and this country, face as we enter into 2018.

I have also founded successful businesses, and throughout any business many negatives, barriers, difficulties and obstacles present themselves, but drive, enthusiasm, positivity and determination always prevailed. I really believe – and it has been proven that by thinking positively, positive things happen – that positive energy changes everything. Cheer up, John. I don't think you are quite ready for the motivational speaking circuit yet, but I wish you a belated 'happy New Year'. We all have a great deal to look forward to, and I can't wait! Now, where did I put those rose-tinted glasses?

Cliff Slade
Tenbury Wells

The next week, I followed up with a positive letter checkmating this Mr Foster guy's previous doom and gloom. Cheer up old mate!

Dear Sir,

Good news!

Tenbury Advertiser (February 8th) was a week full of positive, uplifting Tenbury news that really made me feel good! The front-page article hailed the planned campaign by the Tenbury Wells and Museum group to 'capture the past' and bring history to life using digital media outlets around the town. What a fantastic initiative! Caroline Palethorpe rightly highlighted that Tenbury has a rich heritage, as well as characters and buildings, and don't forget our many pubs.

Within the inner pages, Tenbury Town Band appear handing over an amazing £1088, raised via its charity event in the town and then handing its proceeds straight back into the Tenbury community facility for young people 'Cafe 27'. What an amazing place 'Cafe 27' has developed into over the seventeen years it has been operating. It was heartening to read what this place has to offer. Well done, Lou Taylor, and well done Tenbury Town Band which, in itself, just continues to thrive and be so much an integral part of Tenbury.

We then hear that Councillor Pollock addressed the town council on apprenticeship prospects for our region's youngsters and separately, 'Cadmore Lodge' is again to be a community venue for various family and corporate functions inviting local businesses to engage with them – great news!

On the back page, Tenbury United produced a dazzling performance to beat top of the league, Wellington Rangers – well done lads!

We then read that The Regal, Tenbury's central feature continues to produce and present some amazing shows in our town, and is now entering a period of offering community auditions for its planned 2018 production of 'The Wizard Of Oz' which is a fantastic opportunity for anyone of any age aspiring to tread the boards. With Tenbury town aesthetically looking great at the moment, 'the yellow brick road' seems a rather timely production choice.

Perhaps, John Foster could audition for the Tin Man, who can supposedly only function with the lubricant of Europe within his joints. Me, I'm auditioning for Toto because I am careful and intelligent and prevent people from becoming grey.

Cliff Slade (Toto)
Tenbury Wells

Now back to 1979, and this pure-bred filly presented herself at the starting gate. This Julie Sheldon went about her work at the pop factory being closely stalked by every red-blooded stallion at the factory, including me. Even in those early character-evolving days, and pre-job and business success, I had that natural instinct to win, to succeed by doing something different, something better, but I had to be quick, or did I? That's what all my competition would be doing – something quick. This Julie Sheldon would only be at the pop factory for the summer, and then she would be gone and off to college.

I needed to attract this incredibly attractive, fit filly, so I put into practise my dynamic plan of action that was instinctively right, and I needed to be ready to change as the situation demanded. This was going to be a momentous effort and a master plan as I was punching well above my weight, and as she was single, she could possibly be swept off her feet at any moment by the competition, but I always believed I would be the best, and therefore I would be.

Julie Sheldon had not got a clue who I was nor even gave me a second look, so I needed an introduction to put my name out there, get noticed. Although it would have been different, this was not the time for a letter! Mick Marston (the lorry driver), he bloody lived with her. I befriended him. I repeated, until it was in his psyche, that I was interested in her. He, in turn, mentioned my name in her secure, warm and comfortable surroundings – her home. I was now hypothetically, psychologically and theoretically in her house, in her mind, and I hadn't even met her yet. There then followed the whole summer. Four weeks of us passing each other without any verbal communication, but we were at least fleetingly glancing at each other. I needed extra help. I confided in the drummer in our band, John Greenhouse, who was in communication with her and spoke to her every day. 'Tell her I fancy her, John.' He did and Julie informed John, 'well, he will have to ask me out'. I didn't know whether he was just winding me up and wanted me to make a right fool of myself, as that is what everybody did in a pop factory. Life was just a bloody laugh, particularly with John, a great, close friend who I had shared half of my life with in the band having a laugh! John's mother-in-law was Rene Bridges. Rene came to watch us play at every opportunity, and Julie babysat for her on those nights – another great opportunity for planting some further seeds, this time female-to-female. Back came the same response, 'well, he will have to ask me out!' Me, ask someone out. You must be joking! The girls always asked me, and they did. I had never asked a girl out in my life, and that was one thing in my life I was not naturally wired for! The absolute pain and fear I felt at the very thought of asking someone out was unbearable, not the rejection because this Julie Sheldon had already stated, 'he will have to ask me out', so that wasn't an 'I'm not interested' was it?

Summer was passing and coming to a rapid conclusion, and all the temporary summer staff were served with notice. The following week would be the last week. Time was running out as we entered the last week. Momentum, expectation and screams of 'ask her bloody out!' from John, Rene and now half of my work mates, and now all her mates, and everybody else who worked in the factory much to the amusement of all, rang in my ears. The whole week went by, and I don't think I did any work that week apart from trying to create situations where it was accidentally just me and her, so I could ask her out. I had to do it. I was petrified! It was her last day, Friday, the factory lunchtime and everything stopped. Julie was collecting her two free bottles of pop, and at 3.30 pm she would clock out, never to be seen again!

I could see her outside walking down from a warehouse making her way back to the factory, and I was driving my forklift truck towards her. But there was a major problem because she was walking with her mate. I had to do it now, now, bloody now! I couldn't breathe, and my whole world turned back into that speechless child in class again just like it does every time. Oh my god, the pain, but I had to do it! I had to go through the fear and do it! I drove towards them, and it seemed the whole world was watching; 'is the prat going to ask her?' I pulled up alongside her on my truck, and we looked directly at each other for the first time. As I wrestled to stop, my heart beating out of my jacket, I opened my mouth, just as she dropped one of her two bottles of pop. It was lemonade and it rolled away. Julie scrambled about trying to bring the bottle under control. Oh my god, what a bloody situation to add to my embarrassment; she had dropped her lemonade. Julie picked the bottle up, and thankfully, it had not exploded and headed for orbit, and her mate walked off as she was obviously aware that I was about to pop (excuse the pun) the question. Thank god for that, as it was now just me and her, albeit we were in the middle of the yard and everyone knew my intention. Julie gathered her composure, and for the first and last time, I saw her with a flushed face. Close up she was even more attractive. She was absolutely beautiful, and I felt a strange calm come all over me from somewhere, which culminated in me calmly speaking the words, 'do you fancy coming out for a drink over the weekend?' I did it – the sentence I had been practising for a whole summer and she replied, 'no!'

'No', she said, not this weekend, 'I am going to stay with my sister for a week. What about the following weekend?' Phew! My young, fragile, developing virility ego was intact! The whole factory and my work mates were relieved, and again, it was humorous because 'Joey', my nickname, had finally asked the girl out. Mick Marston wound me up for the week telling me she had high-end restaurant expectations for our first date. I had never been to a bloody restaurant with a girl or anyone. I wouldn't know what to do, what to order, where to go, what wine to order, what to wear, or even which knife and fork to use. She was just sixteen, and I was barely just nineteen; we were just kids, but at least Julie was physically developed. I could see that, but *I* wasn't.

Asking a girl out for the first time, particularly this champion breed, and receiving an affirmative from her, are seemingly normal, small, human, post-adolescent steps, but for me, still that insular, shy and emotionally fragile child, it was like an atomic inoculation shot of confidence and self-belief in my ever-developing personality. For me, that early confidence and belief stayed with me in my relationships, work, business, family and in the way that I wrote. I wasn't afraid to say and write what I thought or believed, or afraid of the consequences of differing views. Of course, I respected other and opposite notions, and I was still that great listener, but I was a confident me. Once confidence is consumed, it emits itself and attracts, and whilst it attracts it grows.

This letter, which went into print, was light-hearted but with a point to make, and it was written with confidence.

```
Dear Editor,
        Fashionable Government Advice.
        I have always considered sensible gov-
ernment advice and was always conscious
that getting married early on would bene-
fit me financially, from a tax perspec-
tive, so I did, and we did! I had a
```

healthy tax rebate, and I gained a married tax allowance! We were then encouraged to produce children – more tax benefits and even a weekly child allowance – so I took advantage and had two, one of each! No one informed me that when child benefit finished at sixteen, this is the time a child becomes the most expensive household expenditure for many years thereafter! Also, we are in our thirty-fifth year of being married, and I now wonder if those early financial benefits offset my health and wellbeing balance today.

A few years ago, I was encouraged to purchase a diesel car rather than a petrol vehicle. Diesel vehicles emitted less CO_2 than petrol, and with the attractive tax breaks associated with diesels, why would any fool buy a petrol-propelled vehicle? Today, I am being punished by paying a premium road tax rate for the same vehicle, as it's considered a health hazard because of the high nitrogen oxide emissions. I am also paying more at the pumps for diesel than petrol and I'm now being encouraged to scrap my vehicle before it gets banned from certain cities. Similarly, we have a fantastic wood burner, purchased on the basis that we were burning and producing clean energy, whilst contributing towards saving our planet's fossil reserves, but Sadiq Khan now wants to

ban the use of wood burners because of air
pollution.

I am currently listening to BBC Radio
driving advice, telling me to only drive
if my journey is absolutely necessary, so
I think I will stay at home today, and do
all my unnecessary driving tomorrow.

As I drink my fourteen units of alcohol a week and eat my five a day, I would
have a big pinch of salt with all this advice if it wasn't so bad for me!

Cliff Slade
Tenbury Wells

No one ever wanted to tackle dog fouling. There are
a lot of dog owners out there, and we mustn't upset them.
Yes, we can, and I did in a proper way, with a bit of humour but to the point – to the point, in Churchillian style.
The Winston Churchill film, *'Darkest Hour'* had just been
released.

Dear Editor,
      Tenbury's 'Darkest Hour'.
      Tenbury Wells Mayor, Mark Willis
(Viewpoint, Advertiser 1st February, 2018),
quite rightly highlights his frustration
with dog mess blighting our town. I concur
but blighting is an understatement; it's
more like an epidemic. The main and side
streets of Tenbury are nothing short of

absolutely disgusting and shameful, and in
urgent need of some serious action! The
term dog mess isn't the correct terminolo-
gy. It's quite simply human muck – muck
left by illiterate, ignorant and irresponsible humans, whom the unfortunate canine
has as a carer!

Tenbury Mayor hails illuminating,
flashing speed indicators at St Michael's
(Advertiser 15th February, 2018). Surely
the same technology is required for these
human street-muckers. These human muckers
only slither around the streets in dark-
ness and in the early hours to permeate
their filthy behaviour, so let's invest in
night vision CCTV, and record them as they
muck the streets without any consideration
for anyone.

This is Tenbury's 'darkest hour'. We
are all fed up and need some strong leadership from Malvern Hills District Council
in our hour of need. At the moment they
are offering us nothing. With all our
might and strength, we must come together
and wage war on the monstrous tyranny of
muckers by hiding in the bushes, hiding
behind the lamp posts, in the gardens and
on the rooftops in an effort to identify
these muckers. We should never give up nor
despair about cleaning up our streets from
these inconsiderate, human muckers. This
is going to be an ordeal of the most

grievous kind. We have under our heels and on our soles, many, many months of struggle, suffering and side stepping!

This is not a war against the high-up majority of people who use long words and have different feelings and are, of course, responsible dog owners. But it has to be said, that never in the history of Tenbury, has so much muck been left by such an irresponsible few, and never has a single letter spoken for so many. 'Come then, let us go forward together with our united strength.' Visit MHDC website and record your observations and individuals to bring this minority of human muckers to justice.

Cliff Slade
Tenbury Wells

Waiting for that week to pass for my date night was like waiting for a lifetime! The Saturday evening arrived, and I shaved the three hairs off my chin. I lashed on the 'Brut' aftershave, put on my flared jeans and chequered socks with my woven red, black and tan horseshoe-shaped shoes. Finally, I adorned my non-hairy chest with a blue, short-sleeved shirt with red and white stripes down the sleeve and on the front pocket. And my plain blue Y-fronts of course! I had cleaned my Ford Escort car and got my Beach Boys and Buddy Holly tapes all primed up in my tape player. Never mind Buddy Holly – I was the boy! I drove down to her house and waited outside and waited and waited! Perhaps I should peep the horn, so I did, and did it again and again, but I was drawing attention to myself. Bloody hell! I haven't got to get out of the car and knock on the door, have I? I bloody had, and as I did the door opened and my god, there she was! Dressed in silver high-heeled shoes which brought Julie almost up to my level with me; cream, tight-fitting corduroy trousers and a pink, silky shirt; immaculately applied but almost invisible make up, with those big, fat lips, complemented by this incredibly dark skin and absolutely jet black, straight, long hair with those amazing cheekbone features she filled me with awe. At the door with her, standing over the back of Julie's right shoulder was her sister, Lyn, straining to have a look at me. Lyn, although older, looked a bit tasty as well. Julie said, 'bye', to her sister, and I said, 'hi', and waved to Lyn who said, 'have a nice time!' I opened the passage door to let Julie through first and got a whiff of an incredible female aroma, and this, coupled with my view of her rear end, only enhanced my now musk state. For god's sake! I literally could not believe my luck. Make the most of this, Cliff, I thought.

As Julie stepped into the car, not only did we commence our first tentative steps in a relationship, but these were the first steps of a life journey we were both embarking on, which would see us both change to the extent that we would not recognise each other from that day to this.

Isn't it strange or maybe fate, fortune or those karma particles drawing us together, that we indeed came together? Isn't it strange that if my mother had had a successful relationship with my father and subsequent second stepfather, I would not have arrived in Tenbury Wells with all my attached childhood pains, tribulations and personal struggles? Isn't it strange that if Julie's mother had not so sadly passed away far too young when Julie was just twelve, presenting her with an unimaginable emotional ordeal at such a critical adolescent stage in her life, she would not have been in Tenbury Wells at the time we came together. Or had 'fait accompli' already sealed and decided our future?

I was five feet eleven inches tall, but with Julie on my arm I grew another foot, and I walked tall. I took her all around my local pubs in Worcester and she was impressed. My mates in Worcester were also impressed but most of all I was. Julie turned heads wherever we went, and in those early days, I experienced a new emotion, the only emotion I really experienced apart from lust! That emotion was a strong, potentially relationship-destroying emotion - jealously! Every young stag, wherever we went, was drooling and salivating all over her, and it was getting to me! Not only was jealousy a wrecking vehicle for our new companionship, it was also so strong that I had to do something about it, and just like everything that presents itself to me, I knew exactly what to do. I thought and looked at myself and the destruction that this jealously could reap and decided not to be jealous, and from that moment I wasn't, ever thereafter. I came to the conclusion that Julie was with me. She had made the decision to be with me, and all I had to do was enjoy every moment of the time we were together. She was well out of my class, so I decided to enjoy and savour the looks she was getting, and the fact other lads were looking at me with envy. I accepted that if it was all over tomorrow, it was a great experience, and I was the lucky one and had grown in confidence. All the other girls around my network would be attracted to me because I had pulled this amazingly attractive, intelligent and classy thoroughbred. Attraction attracts! I was a winner both ways, and with that little transgression out of the way, positivity and an open, trustful and respectful relationship was allowed to flow without any controls decreed. I had to trust her and I did. To believe in myself, I had to trust and believe in her, and I did!

With confidence and jealously out of the way and the ability to laugh at ourselves, this correlation later came out in my letter writing. I could say and write things or refer to Julie, and we would both know the real relationship behind the real us.

This letter was never printed in my local paper, and Julie always allowed me to mention her without any warnings or restrictions, unlike the editor of the day who probably thought this was a bit too fruity for our local newspaper!

Dear Sir,

So many mixed messages and contradictory laboratory studies are confusing me! As a child, any home-fried food was cooked in lard with bread and dripping a welcome bonus. This was considered to be unhealthy and a heart disease risk, and we were then scared into switching to cooking oils such as vegetable oils. These oils are now considered carcinogenic, and we are now informed lard is a healthy option! Great!

The Food Standards Agency now informs me over-cooked roast potatoes, chips, crisps and toast can produce acrylamide which causes cancer. Crikey!

As kids we would choose and fight over the crispiest, darkest roast potato stuck to the roasting pan. Similarly, my toast would be dark and very much well done. Excellent!

The Government's new 'Go for Gold' healthy food campaign now informs me to drop the dark and go for blonde! Whilst studying this advice, I looked across to my wife who is olive skinned and brunette and wonder is she possibly a hazard to my health? Mmmmm!

Being in the twilight of my fifties, the study that really engaged me was the one that claimed that the over-fifties enjoy and experience the best ever intimate moments compared to any other age group. Wahey!

Putting all the confusing food advice aside, I focused on the good and popped upstairs and slipped on my lucky, silky, black boxer shorts and draped myself on the settee. We enjoyed a glass of wine or two and fell asleep. How disappointing!

However, before we got up the next morning the most incredible three events happened! Firstly, the previous evening's lost intimate moment was recaptured which was amazing. Secondly, my wife got up and made me the most fantastic full English breakfast with well-done toast. Thirdly, I woke up!

Cliff Slade
Tenbury Wells

A further small letter that was printed in a couple of newspapers!

Dear Sir,

Besides being a talented English teacher, my wife has just graduated from Worcester University with a postgraduate certificate in nutrition, health and diet,

```
which is great news for her, but terrible
news for me. I now weigh the same as I did
eleven years ago!
```

Cliff Slade
Tenbury Wells

We spent the first year together and never had a cross word. We laughed our way through our adolescent relationship. She was amusing and funny and didn't know she was. There was a naivety about her humour, and she laughed at me and I laughed at her. She needed to spend a penny one evening whilst we were driving through Worcester. I pulled up outside some public toilets, 'the gents' toilets!', I gestured to her, 'there', pointing at the gents. Quickly, off she went straight into the gents. I was crying with laughter in the car, which was just compounded, when she quickly came out and asked me for 5p for access, and off she went back in again! I'm not sure to this day who was having one over on the other!

On another occasion, I sent her to the toilet into the busy kitchen of a pub and watched her negotiate the chefs and waiters through the kitchen prep area. She kept going despite bringing the kitchen to a standstill and to the bemusement of the head chef and his kitchen entourage! We couldn't stop laughing. We were laughing all the time with each other, enjoying each other. We didn't have a row at all in the first year, and something new was now entering my life experience in the form of 'physical contact'. Julie always wanted to be close to me; she wanted to hold my hand, sit with me holding hands, put her arm around me, and put her hand on my knee whilst I was driving. She wanted to kiss me and hug me, not only in private, but also in public. How bizarre! I didn't recognise this weird and strange behaviour. I felt awkward and uncomfortable; this wasn't natural, and I needed to know what this was all about. At this time, 'Google' was still a far-off invention, so I quickly referenced this new phenomenon in my old school dictionary. It was called 'intimacy'. Where did this 'intimacy' come from? I further scrutinised my dictionary, and it informed me that core beliefs are based on deep-seated feelings that we developed in early childhood! Aaarrrgggghhhh! Bloody great! Something to do with feelings developed as a child. No wonder I felt uncomfortable and out of my depth! Intimacy and feelings were not part of me, and I didn't know how to do it and this didn't bode well. I may have needed help but I never needed help in the past; it was time to listen and watch again!

I sat with my limited functional feelings, functional to me as that was the only learnt behaviour I could emit, but to Julie, perhaps dysfunctional, or not! Our two characters' emotional rearing and nurturing backgrounds were coming together. This coming together could potentially conflict or blend – these were early days! For the time being, I mimicked Julie; that's all I could do. I had not felt, experienced or encountered the phenomenon of intimacy that was steadily and tentatively unfolding between us both. Julie gave me a positive physical stroke (steady!) and I reciprocated. Strokes, as in what we may give a dog and then watch the canine's response. Its eyes go all gooey. Its tail wags, it pants and swallows creating a reverberating sound effect that resembles a cross between a woof and a gurgling, yawning gulp, simultaneously generating a tingling, gentle rush of pleasure.

Julie held my hand. I held hers. She looked into my eyes and I looked the other way. She put her arm around me, and I put my arm halfway around her. She said I looked good. I said she looked all right. I said, 'I'll buy these drinks, food etc.', she said, 'OK', I opened doors for her, she walked through them, she moved towards me for a kiss and I let her. It was all OK-ish as I was just impersonating her behaviour, so I was getting by...for now. If I were to pen a little epistle and correspond with myself at this time it would read:

```
Dear Sir,
     I recently met a person who showed me
some care and kindness, both verbally and
physically. Her name is Julie and she is
just sixteen. Julie is not my favourite
name, as the only other Julie I know was
from a great big family on the council es-
```

tate in Worcester, whom I would not associate with being attractive, cultural or desirable!

The Julie I have met is very much the sort of person whom I would very much like to be with, as she makes me feel good – good in the sense she is the opposite gender (wahey!) and good as she is way too good for me, and I am certainly punching above my weight. Unlike me, she is very educated as she has certificates to prove it. Julie has just completed O levels at grammar school and is now going to college to do A levels in German and French! I ain't got none of them, so that means her's cleverer than me, dun it?

As our relationship is developing, Julie wants to be physical and intimate with me in a verbal, public and private sense, which is fine. I am learning as I go along, albeit Julie is more experienced and knowledgeable in these matters, as she has had a very different emotional, inclusive family background. I'm sensing that Julie expects some reciprocal love, but it's a bit difficult for me to express on all fronts because I don't know how to love, or whether I have love in me or understand love. Can a relationship be successful without love? Where is this love? Time has flown, and we have now been together for four years. With a great deal of help from Julie, I, and she, have been very successful at avoiding the word love, the commitment to love and deflecting the affection! In that four years, I have never told Julie that I loved her, and that is probably because life is so fast that time has been taken up with me getting to know Julie's big family and Julie getting to know my even bigger family. For two years, Julie was committed to her studies and then she got a job and took driving lessons. I was working seven days a week and our relationship was, in every sense of the word, now physical, so we were busy pretending to be Mr and Mrs Smith in Blackpool bed and breakfasts and so forth. We were always busy and changing.

I enjoyed paying for Julie's driving lessons, buying her spectacles, buying her clothes and spoiling her for her birthday and, of course, Christmas. I bought Julie a lovely silver bangle for Christmas from a local jeweller, and she still has it today. I had it inscribed with 'To Julie from Cliff 1980'. Now that is love!

Julie told me she had a boyfriend who said she was so beautiful and told her he absolutely loved and adored her. He was always telling her this and it really put her off him, and she gave him the boot. That's a good enough reason for me to hold back on that love business. I was young,

```
strong, fit and powerful, both physically
and  characteristically.  That  is  what  a
girl  wants:  protection,  confidence,  cha-
risma,  security,  stability,  friendship,
belonging  and  that  physical  bit,  and  that
is what I was giving her.
```
Cliff Slade
Tenbury Wells

Unbeknown to Julie and me at the time, our relationship was so successful because Julie was in emotional turmoil and trying to come to terms with losing her mum at the age of twelve! For a girl to lose her mother at such a critical age was life changing, and it was. Within a short period, Julie had moved to live with her sister in Tenbury Wells. Her dad, Tom, had remarried, so she had also now lost her original home and her father to his new wife and child. Julie's family, home and security were broken up, and she also lost her brother, as he moved away to live in London, and his life was also, therefore, in chaos. Julie was emotionally internalising all this disorder, as well as grieving, or not.

As our relationship developed, I learnt Julie's relationship with her father was quite formal. It was rarely physical or intimate, similar to my experience. He didn't verbally say, 'I love you', and the only positive endorsement that she had was when she successfully passed the eleven plus exam and was accepted into Ludlow Grammar School. Her father scooped her up, whizzed her around the room and said, 'well done!' That said, Julie was loved by her mum, sisters and brother and she knew how to love, but a father's endorsement for a daughter's emotional development, well-being, balance and stability makes, breaks, stabilises and defines her character, behaviour and relationships with others – with me!

In the background was also a family tragedy. Julie's brother tragically lost his life at the age of six whilst out playing in rock pools on holiday in Wales. The impact on Julie's father and family needs no imagination. Julie was born soon after this tragedy.

So Julie and I now came together with our dysfunctional but different and similar experiences. This had the potential for disaster, disorder or delight and enlightenment. On the surface, we seemed well-balanced but emotionally, psychologically and intimately, we were miles apart. I was never told I was loved. Neither was Julie (by her father) so how were we going to express our love to each other? Is love a verb or noun? It was time again to do what I was good at – listen, absorb and act!

Going out together is like a box-ticking exercise. Julie wrote a list with her sister as to what she was looking for. She was looking for someone who loved and respected her and had a good relationship with his mother (apparently, I got a tick for that!) I also passed the womaniser, alcoholic, wife-beater and mental litmus test. I also had to be healthy, attractive, well-dressed, kind, have a sense of humour, be a hard worker, generous and a provider, and a little bit of charisma, but at the top of her list, at this early stage, was security, protector, self-assured and able to make decisions, and confident with a potential to build a nest, a home together. Julie knew who I was and what she was looking for before we met! I sensed all this very quickly, and I knew exactly what Julie wanted, as I had switched on my power of listening, observing and tapping into people's inner sanctuary – their mind! I was good at that; I knew intuitively what to do, how to do it and when to do it. I always did!

Similarly, I had a tick list, albeit, a simplified version. At the top of the list was just the lust and desire factor. No doubt, this filly was the top racing horse in the stable (double, treble ticks). Julie was, and still is, a sophisticated dresser and always turned heads. It was often said that she would look good wearing a bin liner, and she would. I was looking for someone who laughed at my sense of humour and could laugh at herself. I needed someone who I could trust and someone who was loyal and committed to me. Trust, loyalty and commitment were so important to me. Those are the three elements I had lost in my early childhood. My trust, assurance and faith were put to the test when I was taken away from my home, lost my mother and put in a children's home. Would it happen again? Would I lose everything again? The difference now was that I was in control this time, and it was my destiny and knew I had found something special because I had stopped looking back. I wanted someone self-confident, stable, reliable and a bit daring. A couple of things happened that completely sealed, endorsed and decided my suitor search. Julie's sister and family went away on holiday and Julie had the house to herself. She invited me for dinner. She was going to cook me a dinner. Julie cooked me the most fantastic pork chop dinner I had ever had the pleasure to consume. Julie was, and still is, a most amazing cook. What is that saying? 'The way to a man's heart is…'. I was completely sold. This wasn't just a flat-racing filly, this one was also a potential national hunt champion! I can remember putting my hands around her waist, and I had, never in my limited experience with girls, encountered such slim hips and fat kissing lips. She really was the full package; we made good use of the house for the rest of the week! Julie was also very daring and edgy. She would do anything if you dared her, whereas I was reserved, shy and a little self-conscious. She didn't seem to have any inhibitions, particularly with her body. She was very confident if we went swimming, she would strut her stuff in her bikini, and her clothes may as well have been sprayed on. Wherever we were or wherever we went, both intimately and publicly, Julie really did ooze self-confidence in herself and her sexuality. This was further endorsed on my eighteenth and twenty first birthdays! Julie was still at college, and money was tight for her. My nineteenth birthday was approaching and so was the Tenbury Carnival Queen competition that carried a £25 cash winning bounty. Julie put on those spray-on trousers and entered and won and I got a birthday present! Similarly, on my twenty first birthday, Julie entered 'Miss Tramps', Worcester's biggest and most popular nightclub. Again, she won, gathering a plethora of prizes which included cash and automatic entry into 'Miss Worcester News'. If she won this, it was a gateway into the 'Miss UK' competition. Julie was interviewed at a packed top hotel, strutted her stuff in her swimming costume and evening dress, and came third. She was robbed, but this girl was for keeps and she was certainly demonstrating commitment and care for me.

At that time, I quickly recognised that the most important elements needed from me were security, stability, protection, communication, hope, balance, reliability, trust, and a settled future. We weren't in love with each other; we were fulfilling a need in each other, weren't we?

Being together for four years came to an end, an end as we got married! I never asked Julie to marry me. Wow, how romantic! Romance is closely associated with love, affection and intimacy, so it necessarily follows that romance is totally devoid within me and Julie! So how did we both agree to get married?

Julie was living with her sister. She moved out and temporally moved into my packed house, and then Julie moved into a room at a local pub. We really wanted to be together and looked at the possibility of buying a low-cost, small property. She was now working in her first job, and I was earning and working all hours, but we didn't have any savings. We just spent it on going out and enjoying ourselves. We looked at a little, semi-detached black and white cottage, decided to apply for a mortgage, and with our earnings we thought we could just about manage it. We booked an appointment for our mortgage application meeting at our local bank and attended a very formal interview with the manager sitting behind his very official desk, with a very large apple placed in the middle, presumably for his elevenses; it really was serious, official stuff. Halfway through our interview, the manager needed to photocopy our earning details and popped into the office next door. Julie and I sat nicely awaiting his return looking, like two little children, at his big, rosy, juicy apple. I turned to Julie and stupidly dared her to have a bite of the apple – big mistake! Before I could utter a repeal of my dare, she had picked the apple up, taken a big bite and placed it back on the table, with the large bite imprint facing us just as the door flung open and the manager returned! I was mortified and perplexed as well as being totally consumed in a childlike frozen, hilarity state, whilst trying not to make eye contact with Julie. We were suc-

cessful with our mortgage application and partly successful at keeping ourselves together. We could not stop
laughing when we left his office, particularly thinking
about him when he discovered a bite in his apple and how
it got there! The only negative consequence of the successful and amusing meeting was a deposit was needed, and
we had no money! I sold my guitar, my amp and my car
to raise the funds for the deposit. The £19k mortgage and
£77 a month mortgage payment were now ours. We were
very excited, and Julie and I had our own home and the
benefits of having our own security and stability!

We started measuring, furnishing and buying sec-
ond-hand appliances and furniture and building our first
home together, and Christmas 1982 was approaching. Julie, whilst visiting her father, mentioned in a nonchalant,
off the cuff remark, that we had bought our first home and
that we were going to live together, to which he made
known his displeasure by gently but positively saying to
Julie, 'I would rather you didn't, love'. That was it, we
weren't moving in together for the time being! Christmas
came and the January sales started, and whilst shopping
in the sales for clothes in Debenhams, we noticed the
wedding dresses were incredibly discounted, so Julie
bought a dress in the sales. If dresses were in the sales
wedding rings must be, and they were, so we quickly invested in two! We had the house, dress and rings and we
weren't even engaged! Back to the sales and I bought an

enjoyment, I mean engagement ring, and we sort of announced our coming together. So that is how we came to get married, without me even asking for her hand from her father or Julie herself!

The date was fixed: forth of April 1983. Looking back at our wedding pictures, I looked about eleven years old. The most profound thoughts of that day and above anything (even getting married), was the constant worry and pain thinking I had to make a speech at our reception. I had never made a speech in my life! The second, most prominent memory was standing at the altar with the wedding march belting out from the church organ and looking back up the aisle and seeing Julie making her way towards me, arm in arm with her father. It was such an incredible sight as she looked absolutely stunning. I had to quickly look away or risk bursting into tears – something I hadn't done since being left at the school gates on my own on my first day! I had to be strong and take control of my emotions before my emotions took control of me! I could not believe this person was making a lifelong commitment to me; she was giving herself to me in a church, in front of our families and friends, and in front of God! That's just a little bit of commitment, and for a slight moment I forgot about my speech!

My speech was very brief and painful as always, and I started with, 'my wife and I'. Everyone laughed and I thanked everyone for coming and all the gifts and that was that. I later carried Julie over the threshold, and we were married in a proper way. Mr & Mrs Slade. Whatever did my dad feel and think, as my proper name was Sampson? He never once remarked on it or expressed a view, but I always felt it was wrong!

At the time of our wedding, Julie's dad, Tom, was Managing Director of a very large company. I allowed myself to imagine working for his company in a very senior role. However, just a few months prior to our wedding day, the company went bust and we ended up paying for our own wedding; my dreams of an office job were in tatters and I was stuck with Julie!

We couldn't afford a honeymoon and we really didn't want one. We had a little cottage all kitted out, and it was a dream come true. We had our own place, and we could do what we wanted, when we wanted, in our own place.

The first year of marriage was not good. Julie said that if she had had a suitcase, she would have left me, but a black bin liner exit was not very sophisticated or practical. We argued, fought and sulked our way through a tough year. We were discovering going out with each other and living together are two very different things. We were testing each other all the time. We were pressing various buttons and living on the consequence of the result. On one occasion we fell out, Julie cooked me a dinner, but I left it on the dining room table and decided to cook my own. I used every saucepan and utensil in the kitchen, as I was not used to cooking. When Julie got up the next morning, she launched all the saucepans and crockery all over the back garden path! I returned home later that day, coming down the back garden path and we later made friends. Julie was very pleased with her initiative of orbiting my remnants out of the kitchen door and the subsequent splash down all the garden path, and she asked me in a satisfied manner what I thought when I returned home, seeing my dinner and pots and pans adorning the garden? 'What dinner?', I inquired. It had snowed heavily in the afternoon and completely covered the plate and its contents, so her intended statement was completely lost in a blanket of the white stuff.

In business, in groups and in relationships there is an expression 'storm, norm and perform'. Certainly, we were in the 'storm' stage. It took at least a year for Julie to understand and come to terms, accept and concede that 'I was always right'. Our relationship, our two very different characters, then started to slowly move to the next phase.

A relationship for me and, I now know, for Julie, is ever-changing and the success of our relationship was based on that ever-changing direction in behaviour, understanding, respect, ideas, aspirations, purpose, intention and the appreciation and awareness of each other's needs, both emotionally, and from both our developing ambitions. Our two characters coming together had now dramatically changed each other; we were both very different people in a short time, living and working together. Our early childhood experiences and events were now starting to surface and at times blended us together perfectly, and at times cause problems and issues that would take a lifetime to address or adapt to. Unbelievably and subconsciously, in those early married days, we both fitted into that 1950s and 1960s stereotypical relationship, based on the Peter and Jane children's reading books. Daddy went out to work and Mummy stayed at home to cook, but it was even more bizarre because Julie also went to work, and then came home to cook, clean, iron etc!

In the background, I was still that child, the one who vowed never to cry again after being dumped at the school gate and left on my own to figure things out. I had lost trust in my mother when thrust into a children's home, and never had the support of grandparents, uncles, aunts, father and siblings. I just wanted to be the same as everyone else, but I was the only one with a disabled sister. I was the only one without a father. I even told some friends I didn't have a father because he was dead. It was just easier to say that, as everybody had a bloody father except me! I was just left on my own, left to sort things out myself, make my own decisions and learn whatever I was doing was right or wrong. I grew up fast on my own. I didn't trust anybody but myself. I didn't effectively communicate with significant others, teachers or friends, because I didn't trust them. I didn't believe them. Trust and respect had to be earned from me. I was cautious and insecure! All those matters resurfaced in that first year of marriage and thereafter – I didn't trust anyone – I didn't care for anyone – no one cared and looked out for me. Although married, I was still on my own looking after myself like I always did. I was with Julie, who was now, understandably, insecure. She needed holding, embracing, loving and a future of stability. Julie had lost so much, her mum, her home, her friends and home town and a bit of her dad. I now had to be even stronger than ever for Julie, but underneath, I was also insecure. I had never lost anyone in my family ever, death was just a word. I didn't know what the death of a family member felt like. I lost my home and my mother, albeit in a different way. Julie needed a robust, dependable partner, not an emotional wreck or emotional baggage. She had her own struggle. She didn't need mine on top. Julie didn't know my story, but our stories would come together, and we would learn each other's individual temperaments and personalities the hard way!

As well as the posturing and experiencing the worst of each other's behaviour, we had some fantastic times in our cottage. Julie's cooking and running the home were absolutely fantastic. Julie is, and always has been, a bit of a Scrooge when it comes to money, food and utilities, unlike me. One evening, I opened our sparsely adorned fridge in our kitchen, and thought I really must throw away that tomato that was displaying a blue and penicillin-looking tendency. However, I overlooked it and thought no more of it. The next day, I opened up my much looked-forward-to sandwich box at our first, well-deserved breaktime, and there was the tomato with a bit of grated cheddar. I was mortified and remonstrated that evening to my embarrassed, newish wife! I worked hard and long hours at the soft drinks factory and without fail my sandwiches for work (after being carefully scrutinised for decaying traits!) and a cooked meal were always on the table. I always worked Sundays as it was double time. I would come home for Sunday roast and smelling that Sunday roast walking down the path, without the pots and pans to trip over, was amazing. The roast lamb's rich aroma beckoned me and immediately evoked my early childhood, nostalgic senses of my mum's cooking. The strong, pungent, minty, vinegary smell linked my carefree secure, childhood garden to the dinner table or the school dinner hall, with that waft of home-cooked food coming from the kitchen, when school dinners were cooked fresh in the school kitchen and dished out, fresh, healthy and wholesome. All this was happening when Julie was also holding down a full-time job that was developing and challenging for her. Julie got promoted and had a nice pay rise. Money was flowing into the house. I never ever thought about money; money to me was always there and it always would be. I always believed I would be rich and as usual I was right, I always was! Rich could be ten pound in the bank or a hundred thousand – it didn't matter the amount, I was always rich. I always had what I wanted because I could see it, feel it, believe it and wasn't afraid or cautious of it. Being rich wasn't a figure. It was where I was and where my partner was right now. However, fast approaching for both of us was a biological urge, a biological urge that was to send our relationship to a different emotional level and meaning. However, before we could embark on the next journey, I needed to come to terms with, and start to recognise and appreciate, who I was, and why I was the person I am. Early in our relationship, I dealt with jealousy by accepting and recognising what I had got and enjoyed it at this moment, every moment. I had now had to come to terms with and embrace Julie and me being one and learning and recognising why we conflicted and why we bonded, but we had come this far, we were married.

Many, many years into our marriage, Julie bought and framed some words that were displayed on our home wall. It was a scripture on marriage, written by the prophet Kahlil Gibran and it resonated and defined the next stage of our relationship: -

On Marriage

You were born together, and together you shall be forevermore.

You shall be together when the white wings of death scatter
your days.

Ay, you shall be together even in the silent memory of God.

But let there be spaces in your togetherness,

And let the winds of the heavens dance between you.

Love one another, but make not a bond of love:

Let it rather be a moving sea between the shores of your souls.

Fill each other's cup but drink not from one cup.

Give one another of your bread but eat not from the same loaf.

Sing and dance together and be joyous, but let each one of you
be alone,

Even as the strings of a lute are alone though they quiver
with the same music.

Give your hearts, but not into each other's keeping.

For only the hand of Life can contain your hearts.

And stand together yet not too near together:

For the pillars of the temple stand apart,

And the oak tree and the cypress grow not in each other's shadow.

Kahlil Gibran

Wow! The next and significant years of our marriage
were so defined and followed the path of these words. We
were together, but we needed our own space and direction, and we so did. We were sharing the same cup but

also did not drink from one cup. We laughed and meta-phorically sang and danced together, as well as being happy alone. We stood together but we did not shadow each other.

We never pretended to be like each other; we were two very different people with very different needs, aspirations and ambitions. We were starting to understand our conflicts, our insecurities, our characters, our emotions and behaviours. We were still in first gear and in the storming stage, but we were respecting and trusting each other just a tad more!

```
Dear Julie,
     Four years of marriage is and contin-
ues to be challenging and certainly not
without trials and tribulations, probably
more of the later at the moment, but when
we are happy we are very, very happy but
when we are bad we are bad.
     Still fresh in my memory is that in-
credible vow and obligation you made to me
in the church. I still can't believe how
you committed yourself to me. Why did you
choose me? I feel so grateful and happy we
are married. I can't believe what a great
cook, homemaker, worker and lover you are.
I can't believe we are now planning to
have children, our children - unbelieva-
ble! Why choose to have children with me?
```

One, two or three? Four is too many, isn't
it?
                                    Cliff Slade

That overriding biological urge for both of us was very powerful, so we decided to try for a child. Everything I did was carefully and intentionally planned to the finite, precise detail and again, I knew just what to do and when! As well as the vision, everything I did was absolutely and carefully strategically planned out, with that dynamic risk assessment quickly followed up with action not words. We put our little black and white cottage on the market as it was too small for a family, and we identified our new family home just a few doors up from our existing home. Our first house and the struggles were left behind, and we sold and moved into our new home with fresh energy and hope. That is what happened because that is what I had decided. It was a big house and we spent a great deal of time, money and effort on making it a family home with a nursery. Now the best bit. I had enjoyed all the practice; it was now time to put the pleasure and practice into action!

Planned and forecasted, sole-earning capabilities re-quired me to increase my revenue, my earning potential. Opportunities were presenting themselves for promotion and advancement at the soft drinks factory. Now was the time for me to advance myself, grow personally, and also increase my income for the purpose of providing for my family. I applied for the next job advancement, which was a chargehand, the first level and lowest level of promotion. I looked around at the rest of the competition. I was the best and I immediately got the job. Within a year, I was the shift supervisor. Within another year, I was the warehouse supervisor over all the shift supervisors. Every time an opportunity arose, I believed in myself, in my capabilities and was far better than all my work colleagues below my level, on my level and above my level. I became ruthless and fearless for the next stepping stone, but I always had respect, appreciation and empathy for my subordinates. After all, that is where I had come from, but not where I was going. I always had a respect for my position. I was put there to represent the best interest and advancement of the company I was acting for, and I was bloody good at it. I didn't suffer fools; I had no time for lazy, inconsiderate, selfish actions or attitudes. I was honest, hard-working and fair, and I expected the same in return. I knew all colleagues working together were all different, and I appreciated and understood that, but this was not a time to cross me because I was on a mission of self-growth and realisation of my dreams and aspirations. I was leaving that insecure, introverted, quiet child behind. I had found and heard my own voice, and it was time to put all that listening into action. All that listening was now about to pay dividends. It was now time for me. I was discovering who I was, but I instinctively knew and believed in working together. Being together we were strong, effective and efficient, and I was being noticed by senior staff and treading on my immediate boss's shoes thereafter. My final promotion, before I fledged the soft drinks factory, was as a manager. I got the manager's job, and he didn't speak to me for the rest of his life. Isn't it strange that people blame or look to place their own problems and issues on someone else, instead of owning them, addressing them or even recognising them? My immediate boss was not efficient or organised and had a drinking problem. It therefore necessarily followed that the department's working methods were akin to his disposition. He was warned on several occasions by senior managers that he smelled strongly of alcohol, particularly after lunchtime. It was also affecting his ability to manage his job and even himself. I was promoted and off he went, blaming me for his demise. I cared for his family and his welfare, but to use the idiom again, I didn't suffer fools, or in this case, cover for drunks. I suppose my point is that I was a person who was intrinsically wired for responsibility and for the reliability, trust and credibility that the word responsible demanded in action, and he wasn't. I was responsible because I respected my decisions, and I had come to the conclusion on my own, as I did as a silent child. I believed my judgement was always right. With that belief, I had inner silent strength and a decisive, dogged perseverance that was attractive. I couldn't be anything but a leader, and I was in a rush and learning and moving fast. I now had a reason to be ambitious: a wife, and now a planned family. These early traits would later give me the foundation to go into business; I couldn't fail and never did!

Everything I did and wanted I got because of my positivity, belief and vision, and this was contagious and rubbing off on Julie. Almost at the first time of trying, Julie, became pregnant. Nine, exciting and worrying months passed – worrying because of a spina bifida half-sister, Judith. Julie had additional tests because of this! Growing up, with a disabled sister in the family from the age of seven, was difficult. It wouldn't now happen to me with my child would it? I hoped Julie would be OK and I hoped that the baby had all its toes and fingers in the right place, and I hoped the baby would be healthy and safe. We really didn't care or have a preference for a gender. We, and everyone, just wanted, like every expectant parent, a healthy baby. Julie was building the nest, and as the time neared, Julie became even more active and was full of energy, glowing and bursting to become a mum. She never sat down for a minute. She exercised her mind, body and soul and was well-prepared, educated, composed and organised mentally, physically and healthily. She really was in peak condition; I was in awe of her strengths as a woman. Her body, even pregnant, was toned and fit. Her mind was focused, psychologically primed and energised ready for motherhood. Julie had books everywhere on pregnancy and motherhood, but she didn't need them; she was a natural, instinctive woman. Julie shared her knowledge and took time to give me confidence and calmness that everything was going to be absolutely fine. Her preparation through eating healthily and physically exercising was, in itself, inspiring and comforting. We had a little scare when the bump went quiet and moved very little, so a doctor's visit and prognosis was almost expected – Julie had to slow down, rest and put her feet up. Julie's race was won, as far as motherhood preparation was concerned. She had won the Olympic Pregnant Athlete gold medal, and I so admired her and respected her tenacity.

My birthday is the fourth of May 1960 or 4.5.6. On the tenth of September 1989, or spookily, 10.9.87, Julie, at the age of twenty-four, went into labour. Julie took control, rang the maternity unit at Worcester, and I drove us over. I was scared and excited, but this was not a time for blubbering emotions. This was as real as real can get. At this moment, Julie needed strength, support and a confident hand to hold, or at this moment, to tightly squeeze! This was about to be seriously life changing! I wondered if it would be a boy or girl – please God, just healthy! I hoped Julie would be OK! Julie's contractions were now intense and she was walking around the delivery room, up on the bed, around the bed, lying on the bed, and on all fours on the bed. The baby needed a monitor to be attached to it as labour was now taking time, and eventually, a drug to speed up the delivery was administered. I held Julie tight and reverted to humour. We both laughed until it wasn't funny, and I was told to f#$* off! There was a lot of activity. Julie was instructed to push and she bloody did – she bloody did, bloody hell, she bloody did, and a baby's head with a mass of black hair was now visible. Then, in what seemed like seconds, the wailing baby was on Julie's chest, and the flood of bonding hormones immediately took effect, and Julie naturally held the baby and said 'hellllllloooo! Oh my god, look how much jet-black hair! Is it a boy or girl?' The midwife took the baby and announced, 'it's a girl'. I don't know why, but I was immediately proud of this howling, hairy-looking monkey with a squashed face! As the baby was being cleaned and her throat being cleared, (not that her lungs needed clearing judging by the high velocity sound being emitted), I gave Julie a big kiss, asked her if she was OK and told her how well she had done. She was amazing, absolutely amazing! After our now scrubbed-up baby daughter was placed in a transparent clinical-type cot at the base of the delivery bed, Julie immediately, or no more than ten minutes after giving birth, got to her feet and walked to the cot to the screech of the midwife. 'Julie, get back on the bed.' What an athlete! How fit and strong was she! Julie just walked, quite naturally, back on to the bed. She had

had no medical intervention, before or after, the birth. Wow! The now swaddled-up baby was passed to her, and we both just looked at the most incredible gift with which we had just been blessed. We both counted fingers and ears, and she even had a nose. This little miracle addition was healthy, fit and absolutely beautiful. We looked at each other and didn't say anything; there was no need to say anything. We just looked at our baby – this little human we had just brought into the world. It was an incredibly overwhelming and emotional moment that was only saved by Julie breaking the silence with those three little words that stayed with us both, forever. 'It's a monkey', she said and we couldn't stop laughing. Our baby really did look like a little monkey! The midwife announced that Julie had now to be attended to, and I was passed, for the first time, this little baby who was my daughter. I had never in my life held a baby or interacted with a baby. I said, 'hello', and held her in my arms and just could not believe it. I was not only holding a little human being, but it was also MY baby – half of me! Her little fingers and hands were minute, she had a perfect little button nose, an impeccably formed mouth and olive-toned skin with a mass of jet-black hair. Immediately, I fell in love and felt protective towards her. I could not stop looking at her; she was absolutely perfect and beautiful. The love bond was instantaneous, and that love was in the whole of the room. I was bursting with joy, and the pride I felt was indescribable. As I kissed her cheek, she smelled so sweet, an aroma I could not describe or have ever experienced. I was flushed with the happiest feeling I had ever experienced. I was going to love and protect this baby, like no other baby had ever been loved and protected before. I couldn't wait to tell the world I had a baby daughter. There was a god and I thanked him and have never stopped thanking him since. I kept saying, 'thank you'. I couldn't stop saying 'thank you!' 'Thank you' was my mantra – 'thank you'. I felt so lucky and grateful and thankful. Thank god they are healthy! How many couples in the world have difficulty or are unable to be blessed with what I had just experienced? How many parents face the challenge of having a health issue with a new born baby? Phew! Thank you, God!

We had a name, a name I didn't really like; it was too different. I never wanted to be noticed and being different was noticeable. I wanted Charlotte as my first choice as this was a more conventional name, but Julie was adamant that it was going to be Bethany, and I wasn't about to challenge such a detail after what Julie had just achieved. My input was her second name Charlotte – Bethany Charlotte Slade 10.9.87.

```
Dear Julie,
     I cannot believe that you not only
chose me to marry, but also chose me to
```

have a child with. The way you prepared yourself, our home and me for this beautiful, perfect bundle is just beyond my belief or expectation. No one has ever given me a gift of so much joy or love, and it is difficult for me to comprehend, believe or put into words the way that I feel. I feel different. I feel love and emotion, love and emotion that I didn't realise I had or didn't allow out. Allowing emotion out to others is risky. Risky because my fragile childhood home experiences might be repeated, and that security might be compromised again. When I left the maternity hospital and drove home on my own, I became overwhelmed with everything. I felt such relief that you and Beth were healthy. A massive weight was lifted from my mind. I felt so happy and grateful. Your entire pregnancy period, right up to that magical, memorable delivery, was blessed with your good health, which was only made possible by your preparation, healthy eating, exercise and mental positive attitude. You were, and are, an incredible strength. Alone, and in the car, I reflected on what had just happened to me. I breathed deeply. I choked back the tears and had difficulty in swallowing. I was swallowing the emotion, the love, the tears, the relief, the fear, the pride. There are no words I know to explain what had just happened to me, or to my heart. I was swallowing my feelings. This was a perfect moment, at a perfect time, for me to embrace you and verbalise my feelings towards you, and tell you how immensely proud I am of you and how grateful and privileged I am. A perfect time to tell you that you are perfect, but I don't know how to. I certainly feel it and will look after and provide for you. You have made me a dad and I can't believe it.

Thank you, Julie, for giving me Beth.
Love you,

Cliff xxx

I got on the phone and started telling Julie's family and mine that we were parents. Julie had a big family of three sisters and a brother who all lived nearby. Julie's three sisters all had children, so Anne, Lyn and Sue were always a great deal of support to Julie, and everyone it seemed was waiting for the announcement. I was unable to inform relatives of the weight, the time, or whether it was a normal birth. 'I don't know', I exclaimed. From the moment Beth was announced to our families, Julie was inundated with love and visitors. I absolutely thrived on telling the world, and in particular, mine and Julie's family. However, I was conscious of the fact that a key member of Julie's immediate family wasn't there to witness, support and endorse this momentous occasion with her.

The person Julie most needed and who meant the most to her, and the person Julie most wanted to share this moment with was her mum – what very diverse sentiments we were both experiencing! I ordered and sent flowers to hospital as well as a bunch of bananas for our monkey! Incredibly, and spookily, Julie was transferred from Worcester hospital, my home town, to Ludlow hospital, Julie's home town! Incredibly again, Julie spent the next two weeks in Ludlow maternity hospital, not because anything was wrong but because that was what happened. Julie was now a well-prepared mother ready for motherhood. It has often been said that Julie has written or influenced my letters. After all, Julie has the grammar school education and I have a CSE grade five in English, but it really is the opposite. I write letters for Julie. However, Julie did scribe this letter without my influence and it appeared in our local newspaper!

```
Dear Sir,
    On Thursday, 10th September, at 3.19
pm, I experienced the joys of motherhood.
Baby Beth was born in Ronkswood, Worces-
ter, with the superb expertise of two mid-
wives. However, being 24 miles away, I
didn't have as many visitors as I would
have liked, so I asked for a transfer to
East Hamlet in Ludlow. I expected a flat
```

refusal but they consented explaining that they rarely transferred to Ludlow.

That was when the joys of motherhood really began! What a kind, warm reception I received there, pampering me like royalty and ensuring I had lunch straight away. I have never encountered such friendly, warm-hearted, sincere people, always willing to listen to our numerous problems, and ready to offer good, sound advice even if it was at the unsociable hour of 3.30 am.

In Ronkswood, I was told a five-day stay there would be sufficient, and I am writing this letter on the seventh day and only feel ready now to face the music.

This is the start that every young mother should have, and I know that because of my nine-day stay in East Hamlet, I will cope admirably and confidently, and will have the energy I need for the exhausting but enjoyable time ahead.

Unfortunately, I was not aware that I could have my first baby in East Hamlet, so I want other expectant mums in Tenbury Wells and surrounding districts to realise that they could not be in a better place with the most dedicated midwives and auxiliaries on hand.

Can you also believe they kindly look after the baby the night before you go

home, enabling you and your husband to go
out together?
      Long Live East Hamlet!
                                    Julie Slade

This was a new beginning in our relationship. We were now a family with a new way of life, and we would never be the same couple again! Bizarrely, in life, no one gives you an instruction manual on marriage, and now, even more peculiarly, we are not presented with a manual for raising a child. The only training we have had is from our own childhood experiences, encounters, parenting love or pain and emotions…oh dear! However, I did have this newly appointed mum in Julie, and I trusted her, and her already demonstrated instinct and natural motherly intuition, but Julie also had her childhood and learnt behaviour strengths, weaknesses, inhibitions and upbringing encounters that would play a factor in our new joint adventure…oh dear!

Dear Beth,
      After nine months of a developing, kicking, moving, lumpity bumpity hope, today, I was privileged and blessed to witness you come into the world. To hear your cry and see you breathe and to smell your newborn body was indescribable. I don't understand what has happened to me emotionally, but I am sure going to learn and grow with you! I am going to try and not be a cyclical duplicate of my parents'

parenting efforts. Unlike my dad, I am going to hold and carry you all of the way, not some of the way. Unlike me, you will feel secure and safe, I promise and pledge that. Already your life and security foundations from a parenting perspective have been solidly laid, but this is a new beginning for us three, so I will do my very best to protect, provide for and love you. Love is difficult for me, but I was determined to love you from that very moment you were handed to me in the delivery room. I could not believe what a small, perfect human being you are. I could not comprehend your tiny little fingers and fingernails. I could not grasp, realise or know how you were a bump one minute, and then this tiny little miracle in my arms the next minute; it is sacred and divine. I am so thankful I have you safe and well and being thankful is the beginning of happiness. I have been broken and damaged emotionally, but I'm going to pick up the pieces with you, us two! You have an amazing mum, and we will be an amazing family.

You have a large family and they all love you to bits. You have great-grandparents, and I will bring you up with their best, inherited genetic traits and traditions, you little monkey!

Love you,
Dad xxxx

We were both natural parents. Julie was a remarkable mother, a real natural, and I couldn't stop kissing and holding Beth. I was a full-on, comprehensively involved, and engaged dad. Wasn't that strange? Was it possible from my background and my emotional, environmental past that I would be able or know how to love a child, or was it that I just wanted to give my child everything I didn't have?

I would never dictate to Julie on her life decisions, nor would I impose my will, judgement or decisions on her, and I was always conscious from the beginning of our relationship that Julie was an individual, just like me, with the right to make her own decisions. I always made my own decisions because of my early childhood experiences. I was always, and still am, on my own. That is all I know, so I do walk alone, and I respected that it was important but also normal for me, that Julie had to be her own decision maker. As a couple in a relationship, and now responsible for our first child, we would always discuss matters and genuinely conclude with a joint evaluation and judgement.

Julie's maternity period was coming to an end, and a decision had to be made as to whether she return to work or become a full-time mum. I never, at any stage, expressed my absolute pain and dread that my new daughter would potentially be put into childcare or a nursery; that would completely bring back all the insecurities of being in a children's home. I never wanted my child to remotely experience any of those events that I did. Beth would never feel insecure and would be wholeheartedly protected and safe with me as her dad. Thankfully, without any input from me, Julie decided on her own that she wanted to give her all to Beth and stay at home with her all the time. Money would be tight, but I would work harder and more hours, and Julie would cook for the W.I. She also started her own business 'Kiddies' Korner' selling baby equipment, disposable nappies and clothes. She would very cleverly advertise for a 'cot wanted'. She would get eight or so calls from people wanting to unload their unwanted cots, and Julie would buy them all up for next to nothing, and then advertise in a different newspaper in a bigger city a 'cot for sale' and sell them all for top price, all of them! This was just one product, so if you multiply all the various baby and toddler pieces of equipment, Julie was significantly contributing to our weekly revenue in the evenings when I was home and able to look after Beth! I was now a salaried, day-working, junior manager.

Beth was growing and great fun. Julie was never at home and they were always out doing something – at the library, shopping, visiting friends and family – and Julie even started a new playschool; they were never at home. When I was home, I would immediately give Julie a break and let her rest. I would push our traditional Rolls Royce

Silver Cross pram with the big springs and wheels around the town and surrounding district with Beth fast asleep – being parents was a full time job! Beth would wake in the night for a feed. I would roll over and Julie would feed Beth always, never complaining and never faltering. Julie loved every minute of motherhood! Beth was great fun and much loved. She found solid food, and I was now able to feed her, which was again a great experience with most of the time me wearing her dinner! Beth crawled and then found her feet right at the time we were to learn of another significant change in our life! Julie was pregnant again, thirteen months after Beth was born. This was very much planned, and we decided that a short period of time between siblings would be beneficial to them and us!

For the second time, we were both in awe of nature's natural phenomenon of this unknown human being growing, kicking, hiccupping and moving inside Julie's stomach. This was different preparation, both mentally and physically. Mentally, we had done this before, so we knew what to expect. We were more relaxed, albeit I had the same health and well-being worries for this new arrival as I did with Beth. Physically, Julie again just absolutely blossomed and was an absolute picture of health and fitness. With a thirteen-month-old, lively toddler to chase around, it was physically hard work for Julie, but again, I was there, very much the supporting, getting-involved dad!

What would this baby be – a boy or a girl? We genuinely did not care what gender this one would be. Again, being healthy was top priority, but surely we wouldn't be blessed with a boy, one of each would we? I again felt so grateful and thankful that we were able to experience this phenomenon for a second time when so many people less fortunate needed help or never were able to experience motherhood and parenting. I only had to look at Julie and she was pregnant! As Julie was now a seasoned mother and this was her second child, Julie was allowed to have this baby, barring no problems, at our local maternity unit at Ludlow, Julie's home town and the hospital where she was born! Beth was born in Worcester, my home town and the hospital where I was born!

On the twenty eighth of July 1989, Julie went into labour and went to the brilliant, already experienced hospital and staffed facility that was Ludlow hospital. Julie was relaxed and determined again, to have a natural birth without any medical intervention. Again, Julie was just as educated and prepared and in tip-top physical and mental condition. No speed-enhancing drugs were administered this time, although Julie, in the latter part of labour, was grateful of gas and air. She was certainly making the most of this aid which perversely amused me, as she was obviously becoming intoxicated on a mild hallucinating trip, but her steely determination was unwavering and with the midwife's timely instructions resonating around the room, 'push', I was again privileged and honoured in witnessing the safe arrival of my second child. Without any prompting, wondering, delay, or before either of us could ask or speculate, the midwife blurted out, 'it's a beautiful boy'. How can the great architect of the universe top sending a healthy beautiful girl and send a beautiful healthy boy, a son? He, too, was bellowing at the top of his voice announcing his own arrival, which, in itself was an important, reassuring and comforting din. We had a pigeon pair, the ultimate goal, one of each, a complete family at the first attempt, and I, again, could not stop repeating, 'thank you' into the cosmos. Whoever I was grateful to, I just kept saying 'thank you'. I waited in the time-honoured third position for my opportunity to welcome my son into the world. First was Julie who held, kissed and wondered at this marvel, this little marvel, this time with a tail! Then he was whisked to a nearby preparation table, cleaned, assessed and treated before being presented to me. I held him for the first time and looked into his eyes. I could see an innocent me. From my photographs, I recognised me when I was a baby. He was definitely my son. Again, I was in wonder of this new, little, perfect human being. I had a son. I was so humbled and lost in the magnitude of this significant moment. I felt the responsibility towards this little person. I held his hopes and dreams in my arms, and again I consciously pledged to be with him for the rest of his life, all the way, every step. I want to hear you call me 'Dad' and I want you to know me for as long as our lives last. I want to do everything together. I want for you everything that I didn't have. I'm going to love and hold you. I'm not perfect, but I will try my best.

Julie and I both agreed from the onset that if we had a boy his first name would be Christian. I had an emotional affiliation with a song, '*You Were on My Mind*' covered by Crispian St. Peters. It was a song in 1966 that resonated an emotional, turbulent time for me in the sixties. Crispian was a strange name. I didn't do strange names, so Christian would have been my attachment to that time and song. His middle name would be Michael. My middle name was Michael, Julie's brother's name was Michael, and I had an Uncle Michael. However, our first-choice name was hijacked, and we announced to the world 'Michael Christian Slade', born twenty-eighth of July 1989. Sorry Dad, Slade was entered on his birth certificate!

I left the hospital, this time choking back the emotion of pride and excitement. I had a son. How perfect was my life, how positive and powerful I felt, how thankful and grateful was I, and how happy and content was I! I couldn't believe it. How lucky was I! Was it luck, or had I manifested my family destiny with positivity and the belief that everything will work out? Everything always did work out. It always did, I believed it would and it did!

Dear Michael,

To have a brother for Beth, to have a son for your mum, and for me, as a father, to have a son, is not only magical but also emotionally indescribable. I held your little fingers and you grasped my hand. I was comforted as I watched your little mouth expel and inhale air, and I marvelled at the miracle in my arms, overwhelmed with love and pride. The pride element is easy to feel, but the love is work in progress for me. At the moment, I can't stop kissing and cuddling you, and I won't ever leave or not be there for you. I have a great football team for you to support and watch. You will be a great footie player because I'm going to take you to the park and have a kick about with you. I'll be a full-time, protective dad and you have an incredibly strong, special mum. Your sister, Beth, has a big gob. I brought Beth to your hospital bed to meet you for the first time; she absolutely loved you for all of two minutes. Our life together, for all of us, is going to be a great journey.

Love you,

Dad xxxx

Bringing up two children is the hardest thing I have ever done in my life. The first couple of years with these two little monsters/gifts were exhausting but equally exhilarating. Every step of the way, every day, was a complete privilege. I took every moment to kiss, play, bath, wash, clean, feed, hug, walk, hold, chase, hide, find, watch, protect, trust, provide, sing, read, cry, encourage, laugh, sleep, worry, nurture, nurse, support, guard, provide, listen, advise, learn and take care of them both in equal measure.

Very early on, Julie and I made a sensible pact. We would support and maintain, whether we agreed or not at the time, that whatever advice or reprimand we dished out to our children, we would totally support and be in unison in our decision to show a united front. We would then later further discuss our action and adjust accordingly. At the forefront of our collective decision, we would always listen to the point of view of our remonstrating child but in the background, without a child raising manual, we were not only the product of our parents, but we also had our own positive aspirations as well as emotional deficiencies that would be either passed down or recognised and modified.

One main feature drawn from my childhood was those special Christmases and birthdays. As Beth and Mike grew up, the build-up to Christmas was protracted, intense and extremely exciting. I would wind them up about Father Christmas for weeks. I would walk them around town to see the amazing town Christmas lights with horse-drawn Father Christmas procession. I read to them every night, ratcheting up the anticipation, "Twas the night before Christmas, when all thro' the house | not a creature was stirring, not even a mouse;' I can still recite the whole story without a prompt today! I would decorate the house and adorn the tree in secret, and they would walk into the house or down the stairs the next morning as if Christmas had just magically arrived. Every Christmas I had a tradition and a ritual whereupon we would put a carrot out for Rudolph and a mince pie for Father Crimbo, and Beth and Mick would carry their pillow cases up the stairs with such excitement and expectation that they were almost bursting. When they woke up presents were over-spilling the sacks. Michael was almost twenty six when he realised Father Christmas was not real!

Birthdays were always special, and Julie always had a party for them and, without fail, she made a homemade cake which was not always a design success, but she always got away with it. Those cakes, parties and Christmases are now etched in our children's recollection, their nostalgia-recall cells.

I never stopped kissing them, hugging them, playing with them, supporting them, providing for them, being there for them, protecting them and caring for them. I wanted them to know and experience that I was their dad.

Beth and Michael grew so quickly. It's such a well-versed comment and never made sense or was never noticed by me, but today it's so true, 'where did my, not so much, carefree childhood days go?' But more to the point, today, 'how did our children manage to grow up so fast?'

'Where have all of those years gone?' It is probably a question we all, at some point in our life, particularly me, now question, and I somehow know that I am not alone posing that question, 'how did we, and they, grow up so fast?'

Our children's lives and our triumphs and tribulations with them is a novel and chronicle in itself – sometimes a fairy tale and sometimes a nightmare, but always a joy, privilege and a pleasure to be fifty per cent of their parenting and one hundred percent of their life. I wonder how they will judge my parenting, and I wonder how my actions and behaviour have influenced their character, temperament and personality. I can honestly say that, good or bad, everything I did for them was for love and to the best of my ability.

As they become adults, my physical and tactile love, as in, my capability to give hugs or kisses or affection, regressed to my childhood. Me, as a child, or as an adult, to this day, never kissed or hugged my siblings or parents. NEVER! It's just something we didn't have or do or know. I miss the intimacy that I had with my children today. It's awkward and I have a clear strategy on how to carefully avoid that intimacy because it's not natural to me. It's difficult and of course, that 'it' word is the ability to show and say 'love'. It's not something I have. It's strange. I was determined that my children would be kissed and hugged to death by me. As little children, I didn't want them to experience that lack of intimacy and love from a father.

I know this is a bit freaky that I seem to walk around my home reflecting, acting and living my life off framed scriptures around my home, but this framed body of writing adorning our wall within our home, sums up the gift and message of our children.

On Children
Your children are not your children.
They are the sons and daughters of Life's longing for itself.
They come through you but not from you,
And though they are with you yet they belong not to you.

You may give them your love but not your thoughts,
For they have their own thoughts.
You may house their bodies but not their souls,
For their souls dwell in the house of tomorrow,
which you cannot visit, not even in your dreams.
You may strive to be like them, but seek not to make them like
    you.
For life goes not backward nor tarries with yesterday.

You are the bows from which your children as living arrows are
    sent forth.
The archer sees the mark upon the path of the infinite, and He
    bends you with His might that His arrows may go swift and far.
Let your bending in the archer's hand be for gladness;
For even as He loves the arrow that flies,
so He loves also the bow that is stable.

                                        Kahlil Gibran

Unbeknown to us, on our journey with our children, these words and their message was a natural, albeit not a perfectly exercised, mantra we, as parents, recognised and followed with its significant meaning. It is a fact that no person, particularly our children, belongs to us. Yes, they have our genes and they are a reproduction of our image, but they are a unique, separate entity, just like those little fingernails and fingerprints that I marvelled at in the delivery rooms. I, we, were blessed with children with a blank canvas. It was up to us as archers to send those arrows as children into the future – a future that we must respect was theirs alone. It would prove easier said than done, and life with them was a constant joy, as well as a challenge on a backdrop of our own life experiences. However, as the archer, I hope that I managed to provide a good stable base and foundation to launch those two arrows in a straight and narrow, free-falling line!

I am proud of many things in life that I have achieved and been involved with, but nothing beats being a father. Collectively, with Julie, I am humbled and privileged to call them my family.

In the same way I marvelled at my children as they came into the world, I also marvelled at every step they made in their lives as they developed and negotiated the various stages of life into adults.

Dear Beth,

I have known you all of your life and been lucky and fortunate to have been with you every step of the way. It has been, and still is, mind-blowing observing your nature and personality develop. I watched you in nursery and infant school taking your first tentative steps, and then into junior school where you were a sweet, self-conscious, quiet, apprehensive, popular, beautiful, admired, caring and friendly little child. In no time, you started to shine and blossom, as I proudly came to watch you on stage in front of hundreds of people when you played your clarinet, played the piano, sang solo, sang in the choir, danced and acted in school, theatre pantomimes and drama productions. You were far the best mushroom and pepper pot in those town theatre pantomimes. What a proud moment when you were successful in being awarded the lead role in 'Dazzle' in your final year at school. What a proud moment as I watched you sing, dance and act in that production! Who was that little, Chinese guy in the play?

I look at you and see my image in you. You look like me, but you also look like your mum, thankfully, with her slender, toned and healthy, fit figure. Like me, you do not tolerate fools; you are direct, courageous and adventurous and you have an incredible strength and self-belief and self-worth. You know exactly what you want and where you are going and when. To watch you live your life to the full, with humour and humility, is amazing.

I can't believe we let you breed those rabbits as two became six! I can't believe after so much remonstrating and pleading from you, we bought you a pony, just as you became interested in boyfriends, and I was left feeding and mucking the mule out! Thank goodness I never remarked on those early boyfriends and allowed you to find out yourself who was right and who was not so right! Thankfully, I didn't challenge you too much for smoking and allowed you to experience and learn how such a habit would impact on your health and well-being!

I regret grounding you, telling you off or even telling you what to do; it never ever worked and always had the opposite effect, but I quickly realised that and adopted the only worthwhile and workable solution – let you decide and learn yourself as long as your safety was not compromised.

I am so proud of your educational achievements, your musical grades, your degree, your teacher qualification; you certainly have your mother's academic chromosome.

Second to holding you in my arms, the greatest and most memorable gift that I am blessed and fortunate to have ever experienced with you, was walking you down the aisle and handing you over to your husband, Charlie, for the next chapter in your amazing life. You are now an incredibly caring, considerate and loving mother, and that love towards your children clearly oozes out with reverence and affection and surpasses that which I was determined to provide for you. I am so proud of you as a mother to your children and a wife to your husband. You and Charlie have blessed me with three of the most lovable, beautiful and adorable grandchildren anyone could ever wish or dream to have been blessed with. I find Scarlett, Jasmine and Hugo easy to love and they mean the absolute world to me, just as you do. You are a clever, intelligent, sensitive, loving, balanced and thoughtful, powerful woman with a great sense of purpose, belief and character. I like the person you are. I like the way you make me feel happy, your values, your honesty and integrity, your personality and most of all I am proud to have you as, and to call you, my daughter.

Love you,

Dad xxxx

Dear Mike,

I look at you today and wonder how you managed to grow up so quickly. Yesterday, you were that little person who depended on me and doted on me as I doted on you. I drove a fire engine for eleven years so I could be your hero. I started a football team and football training every Sunday morning with you, so I could be your Alex

Ferguson. I became a business man, a magistrate, a policeman, a Freemason, a football director, a politician, a president and a musician to show you everything and anything was achievable and possible, but most of all, I became a father, a dad, a dad I never had. That for me is the most important contribution that I could ever bequest to you or wish for you, although you will have to judge how valuable and how successful maybe, I was or wasn't at it!

Throughout our time together, I have seen you grow with me, together with your friends and acquaintances, into a genuine, loyal, honest and such a funny, amusing person greatly admired and loved my me, your mum, family and your friends alike. It really is strange how your personality absolutely mirrors your mum's, and yet you look the image of me as a child. You have always been a gentle, thoughtful, caring, measured individual just like your mum. Unlike Beth, you didn't need any time to warm up in confidence, as you were an immediately, confident and self-assured individual with an instant belief in yourself. You had no fear or inhibitions, and you were always up and at the front and first to try or be something. I loved it when, as a toddler, you quietly snuck up to the side of my bed, quietly sneaking past your mum's side, as you always knew I would pull back the duvet to allow you to snuggle up to me in bed, much to the aversion of mum's sensible and organised sleeping rules and routine!

Just like your sister, Beth, you always got involved with school and theatre productions but how amusing that you always got the better part, much to Beth's annoyance, but she was always secretly proud of you getting the part of little bear in the pantomime production of 'Goldilocks and the Three Bears' and also Gretel in 'Hansel and Gretel'. Beth did catch up with you in 'Dazzle', and you were relegated to that little, Chinese guy but equally an amusing and a significant part. You have an amazing, clear, precise and articulate ability to speak, and your voice is certainly a hidden attraction for any such related occupations or interests.

I, and we, have always been amused at your ability and special gift to charm everyone in every situation. You really are blessed with charm and charisma which is an attraction to your perfectly balanced character. I was so proud that you made the bold decision to leave university as it wasn't for you; it's harder to make a decision to leave a situation than it is to stick it out. I felt so anxious but equally excited for you when I waved you off at Heathrow Airport when you decided to travel around Australia and surrounding countries for a year. What a brave and courageous adventure to embark on at such an early age! How on earth you have developed as such a talented and adventurous cook I don't know, but your food is amazing!

You have made me so proud to have you as my son. I love you to bits and even more importantly, I like you. You are a great, generous and loving person. I do miss the child you used to be just because I don't hug or hold you today, but perhaps you're a bit big for that now. I do, however, hope you will eventually stop coming into my bed now you are twenty eight!

Love you,

Dad xxxx

Beth went to university first, followed a year later by Michael because of the obvious age difference. The very day they both left for university and packed their bags and fledged to their respective universities, we both danced and danced around the kitchen floor whooping and laughing with ecstasy that our job was done. We had done our bit. Apparently, there is a psychological study that states that if you can release your children without any regrets, doubts, sadness or woe, then you have done a good job bringing up your children. We certainly did not have any child fledging inhibitions, and we both felt remarkable and looked forward to our life together again. Financially, they were still very attached to us and not quite off our payroll, but this was the first step to taking time out again for ourselves.

My relationship with Julie and her relationship with me was forever changing every step of the way. We didn't recognise the people we were, but we certainly understood the changes and why those changes were slowly, but sometimes very quickly, emotionally and personally altering our personalities and the way in which we behaved and interacted with each other.

We walked and we talked a lot. Walking was time for us to let a bit of ourselves out, more Julie than me, and unbeknown to me at that time, I was a natural cognitive behaviour therapist. Julie would present a topic, subject, issue or problem, and I would just listen. Listening was an art, and I believed everyone knows how to solve their own problem, so it was easy. I just shut my mouth and opened my ears, and Julie would conclude and solve and move forward with whatever problem she was presented. It is a natural human communication trait with friends, family or partners that when someone asks for help we all have the answer because we think we know better and everyone says do this, do that, that happened to me and I did this and that, and ultimately, it either doesn't work or it makes the problem fester or worsen. My approach was listening, just listen, just listen and when Julie put forward that well-versed, lifelong question, 'what do you think I should do?' I would ponder and ponder and say nothing apart from 'what are your options?' Julie would know the options because it was her problem. I would then facilitate her playing out those options, testing them and verbally role-playing them out until she selected the most workable choice. Without fail, Julie's problem or issue was always solved because it was her chosen strategy to correct that particular challenge. She owned it and was taking responsibility for herself. This tactic was also regularly used with our children and in my work place as a manager. Everyone knows how to solve their own problem if they are allowed to speak, and if we do nothing but listen! With this approach, I was becoming more successful in my work, business and relationships.

When Beth and Mike were around five and three years old, understandably, Julie wanted to perhaps explore further education and perhaps further her career prospects. I use the word perhaps, because perhaps Julie didn't recognise at the time why she embarked on this path of enlightenment. As well as teaching English and French at a private school, Julie wanted to fully and comprehensively engage in this potential teaching career. Julie was well-qualified and signed up at university to study a degree course in English literature and language. With two children it wasn't going to be easy, but she was motivated and had the drive and ambition to succeed. I would take over the responsibilities of Beth and Mike in the evenings as they were now starting school and nursery school respectively. The only part in my children's upbringing that I never ever took part in and did not ever do once, was to take them to school and drop them off. Perhaps it was my experience of being dropped off at school on my own. On that day, I was left alone to cry and find my own way in the world of school. I feared Beth or Michael turning to me as I dropped them off at school and being upset because if they did they would have come straight back home with me. Or did I fear not being loved by them? I didn't take them to school for the whole eleven years of their infant and primary schooling!

Julie worked hard and studied hard. She gained an English honours degree and then went straight back to university to train as a teacher and did a further year teacher training (PGCE). On conclusion, Julie then entered the state secondary school system as an English teacher, and proved to be an excellent teacher in various schools and gained many accolades and respect, particularly with students who needed extra help and with particular learning requirements.

As life and our relationship moved on, our talks always exposed our decisions and choices in life. As a child, Julie's most memorable moment with her father was passing the eleven plus exam and being accepted for grammar school. When her father, Tom, came home and learnt of this, he picked her up, spun her around and said, 'well done, love!' She pleased him. She had a positive stroke from a father who was distant and not tactile but highly intelligent and a professional all his life. He also went to grammar school and Julie was his youngest child, and the only one out of four children to be successful at the grammar school exam and selection process.

Julie started grammar school, but this time was sadly going to be tainted with, not only Julie's mum being ill for some months, but also the untimely loss of her mum at a critical age. Julie, understandably, went 'off the boil' at school as she suppressed, not only the grieving process but also the breakup of her home, her father remarrying and Julie going to live with her sister, her brother moving away to London with all his similar troubled and unbalanced emotions deeply concealed.

Through talking, walking and living with each other's behaviour, it was becoming apparent that Julie was working on her degree, teacher training, PGCE and subsequent teaching far too intensely, verging on the extreme. Everything she did was deep, passionate, concentrated and, to the extent, that it was having a mental and physical impact on Julie's ability to function properly, and also, her interaction and relationship with me and Beth and Mike was affected! Julie was making things difficult for herself. She needed to accept second best or the fact she may fail. We explored this behaviour and Julie concluded that her excessive efforts and behaviour were because Julie was doing everything for her father, not for herself. She wanted to recapture his attention, his endorsement, his approval, his love. Julie wanted the moment again where she was spun in his arms. Julie wanted to make him proud of her again with the best possible effort from her, rather than the closing days of her lacklustre grammar school efforts. She wanted to be successful for her dad but also the other significant male in her life...me! Recognising this behaviour, and accepting who she was, where she was, and that she was loved, helped Julie to accept herself and tentatively understand the intensity of everything she was involved in, particularly our relationship. Julie, still today, always will put intense effort into everything she does but recognises and accepts why, and is able to allow herself to be second or accepted for what and who she is, not what she thought her father expected of her; it was OK just to be comfortable with herself.

As already mentioned, just one facet of my emotion is that great pain and awful disposition that I feel when I stand up and speak in front of people, albeit I feel the fear and do it anyway. That pain, that feeling never goes, and is always there. Although I have a strategy to deal with that raw, uncomfortable pain, it still does hurt. Similarly, but on more of an emotional and poignant level, Julie was sadly to lose her dad, but not before he saw Julie successfully embark on her degree to become an English teacher. Julie accepts her dad's endorsement of her achievements, and he was indeed proud of her but that constant reinforcement is always being played out in different aspects of Julie's life, even though she is aware of its emotional source.

Julie was very close to her brother, Michael. Michael returned to the area, got married and had four sons. He also had a son from another relationship. He was a deeply wounded and troubled individual, and Julie always included Michael and his family in gatherings and occasions, but further sadness was to fall on Julie's shoulders and Michael passed away whilst being nursed by her at our home. Michael's wife, Toni, asked me if I would say a few words at his funeral – not again, oh no! But I had to –

somebody had to, for his family, for Julie and for Michael. So, with great pain, again, I rose to my feet!

Imagine as a child growing up as the only boy in a family of four sisters. I'm not sure if that is a good thing or a bad thing, but one thing is for sure - Mike's sisters Anne, Lyn, Sue and Julie surrounded him with love, security and care, and he was much loved by them and his mum and dad.

Mike's masculinity wasn't compromised as he grew up in Ludlow; he was very popular with lots of friends and was known as 'Shelley'. He played in a group and attracted lots of female admirers. If Julie ever mentioned that her brother was 'Shelley', they immediately wanted to be her friend.

I met Julie in 1979 and this is when I first met Mike. He was living and working in London. We immediately formed a bond and from that day to this, we always had a laugh about something. Mike was a man's man, a lady's man, friendly, had a great sense of humour, good looking, with a cockney accent from Ludlow.

The draw of his family and his roots eventually brought Mike back to Tenbury where he worked and lived with his older sister and us. I seem to remember he didn't pay any keep. When I broached the subject of keep, Mike disappeared into the Welsh valleys, and it was here he met a young, attractive, Welsh bar girl by the name of Toni. She was twelve years (old) his junior. When I first met Toni, I thought he was punching well above his weight. Mike really was the cat with the cream and twenty one years ago they got married here in Knighton. Mike embraced married life and would regularly cook the family meals. He was a talented cook, and his meals were prepared and dished out with love and care.

How strange that Mike had four sisters, and then went on to have his own family of four sons - Lewis, Jack, Harry and Andrew. He loved them to bits and they loved him. I have never known Mike have any football experience, but every weekend when Lewis was playing football for Knighton, Mike would turn out and be shouting and screaming tactics and instructions as if he was Alex Ferguson. Perhaps that is the reason the three boys didn't really take up football after that!

Even recently, Mike's humour was always with him, and so was his ability to be careful with money.

Whilst Michael was in hospital being tended to and fussed over by Toni and Julie, Michael fell into a deep sleep. Julie and Toni were left talking and the practical subject of finance came up, and Toni happened to mention she was in need of some money from Michael. Julie was aware that Michael had a great big, fat, loaded wallet under his pillow. It was a big fat wallet because Michael had just received a significant financial settlement from his pension fund. Julie immediately slipped her hand under the snoring Michael's pillow and unloaded a couple of hundred pounds and handed it over to Toni. Toni quickly left the hospital to do practical things with the welcome wad of cash. Michael awoke and Julie informed him what she had done. Flashing and alerting sounds were emitted from his monitoring equipment, and the coronary unit was put on standby as he came to terms with his lower pillow.

I have got to say whilst Mike was in hospital, Toni and Julie were with Mike every day. Julie's love and determination for Mike to recover and get him out of hospital was endless. Everyday Julie took him home-prepared power food. Breakfast, lunch and dinner, he was fed ample amounts of Julie's homemade chicken broth and then more chicken broth!

The day before Mike was due to come to our house, and on a rare occasion Julie was not with Mike, he pulled me close to him and said, 'PLEASE CLIFF, NO MORE CHICKEN BROTH'.

He then pulled me even closer and said with a stronger voice – 'GET MY MONEY BACK FROM TONI'.

Mike would be so happy to see all his nephews and nieces here today – 'when we least deserve to be loved is when we most need to be loved'.

The last couple of years have been very difficult for Rena and Dave, but the greatest challenge was for Toni. Toni, throughout the good times and the challenging times, you have been loyal, caring, understanding and supportive and far exceeded those wedding vows and promises you made with Mike all those years ago. Not only are you a super mum, you were also a super wife.

Mike's real legacy is his four sons. They are a credit to him and themselves and they really are lovely, intelligent and sensitive boys. Your dad loved you and was very proud of each one of you.

We will all miss him...

A constant cause of conflict between Julie and me which took some understanding was that Julie influenced, chose, and bemoaned almost everything I ate and drank. It was carried out in both a subtle and direct way and was of course a manipulative, controlling oppression that was in discord with my philosophy and way of my life. I was a very strong, independent person and very capable of selecting my own food and drink. This was also impacting on Beth and Mike as well, and they were also suffering the same consequences as me. It was time for a walk and talk again! Although we walked and talked, it was several, in fact, many years, from the onset of her behaviour and my reactions to it – so many that we endured a long period of time in conflict over this controlling behaviour. We were both blind as to the reason it was occurring until we walked and talked and kept walking and talking – until we could uncover this reason for this seemingly, endless and seemingly, impenetrable barrier.

Julie was carefully and subconsciously controlling me for a reason; there is always a reason for our behaviour. We knew that. We always knew our behaviour was linked to an emotion, a fear, a love or an experience we perhaps didn't want to repeat or lose. We talked and walked and unlayered uncomfortable places that Julie had been. Julie had everything – materially, financially, a career, children, husband, family and a home, and so did I. Even with a seemingly idyllic world, we were all suffering but none so much as Julie. Why did Julie control my eating? The obvious starting place was to ask her, and she said, 'I want you to eat healthily,' she said, 'I want you to *be* healthy'. Julie was insecure if I didn't eat healthily, if she wasn't in control of what food I digested. Julie was vulnerable because she feared something. Julie feared losing me. Julie feared being left again. Julie feared losing the person she loved, and also Julie feared loving me too much in case she lost me, lost the person she loved. She did not want to go back to that dark place where she had been when she lost her beloved mum, when she was only twelve years old. I was starting to also recognise that perhaps some of my actions and thoughts were also similar to Julie's. I was, perhaps, further complicating our relationship with similar behaviour. I maybe had a fear to love or inability to love because I have, too, albeit, temporarily, suffered the loss of my mother and home. Was I just as big of a problem in this matter as Julie?

I wonder whether I had shut love out at an early age and had closed myself to it. It must be there because aren't we all about 'love'? We are always struggling throughout our life to regain that love that we have lost when acts of unloving behaviour or heartbreak happens to us. It's like an eternal searching for the love that we have lost from our creator and we are seeking the light (love).

Did I, did Julie, have a deep down fear of showing our love to each other because we are all love until we have a significant turmoil or tragedy? We then perhaps learn how to not feel it because of the act of feeling unloved and what has happened to us. Were these the first experiences of receiving fear or an unloving act? Now, throughout our lives, we will never allow ourselves to feel love because that makes us feel vulnerable; it would put us back in that unloved, vulnerable place that we found ourselves in. Or it might be taken from us again, so it's better not to feel love and allow ourselves to be loved. My mum was absent, the absent parent at my most crucial, painful time, and Julie also lost her mum forever, so that was the most painful place Julie could have been in or ever experienced.

We had found a little bit more of ourselves. We had unlocked both our fears and inhibitions on this matter. We discovered that we were both in conflict with each other for the same reason. Just like all our realisations and discoveries in our life and relationship journey, those fears are always there, and they never go away but understanding and recognising our behaviour and fears helps us to live a more harmonised life, emotionally, psychologically, spiritually and mentally.

From time to time, but very rarely, I write a letter to Julie – not emailed, not typed but hand written. This is one of those occasions, an anniversary occasion, where we both exchanged letters independently, not knowing that we had written each other a letter or what the respective contents were.

`Happy Anniversary'.
    Thirty-two years plus four years equals thirty-six years – just seems incredible! I really don't look back and dwell on the past for

good or bad, however, 'anniversary' by its definition I suppose, means the day in which an
important event happened the previous year. So,
on this occasion, I will allow myself to be re-
flective on our thirty-six years, but also
briefly, as it's 'now' that means anything.

I know that I don't say I love you and I
know that I don't kiss and hold you enough, but
that love for you, inside me, is as strong today as it was as our relationship developed all
those years ago. However, it's such a shame and
well-documented that it's difficult for that
feeling inside me to come out and be expressed
as some form of loving expression you deserve –
such as those three magic words or those kisses
and cuddles you wish you could receive more of.
I can only say everything that I do is done out
of love for you, and the love, trust and respect that I have for you today is as strong,
if not more so, than it was when we first met.

Love, respect and trust are three elements
amongst millions of elements within a complicated, protracted relationship, but these are
so important to me. I do love you in the afore-
mentioned way. Respect spills over to many
things, more recently to your comments to my
previous Messiah scripture, 'I will be more
chilled now we have moved'. I know I haven't
and although I haven't shown it, I do respect
your hard work that you put in every day, cooking great food, your job, pacifying me, looking
after Scarlett and Jas, running the house,
cleaning etc. Respect also encompasses respecting you as a person – your individuality, your
nature, your character, your choices, your

great ideas, your strengths, and your intelligence etc.

Trust. I have always trusted you, and you have never ever let me down - never!

I am so happy where we are and more importantly where I am. That can only be achieved by having the freedom and opportunity to be independent 'like "what" you have given me'.

Much discussed, we allow each other to grow and develop, and this is a gift to each other which I hold dearly.

I believe in you and trust you. Perhaps you need to discover that belief and trust in me again.

I love the quotation we both smiled at yesterday 'great men have great weaknesses'. I am great, so it necessarily follows!

I reflect at times. Those odd times when you least love me are probably the times I most need to be loved.

Love you,

Cliff xxxx

My darling Cliff,

Wow, thirty-two years today we vowed to love and stay together, and we went out together for four years before that! Where has the time gone? They say time flies when you're enjoying yourself. I can honestly say I've never had a dull moment. We've always challenged ourselves to push the boundaries, be fulfilled in our work, and always leave enough time to enjoy each other's company. I really do have the perfect life. It keeps getting better.

I hope you think your life is good too. I am less controlling about your food, and it feels quite a relief not to worry about what you're eating. Good job I'm working so that you are free to choose what you eat, and you don't have to eat my concoctions all the time. I do think it's funny when you announce after a few days of my being on holiday, 'ooh, I think I've lost weight!'

After all these wonderful years, I hope you know you are adored and cherished by me, and I do believe more than ever the 'law of attraction' was working in 1979 when we first met. I wrote a list in that year that I wanted somebody who wasn't a drinker, a philanderer, a wife-beater, a gambler or a drug addict. I can't remember what else I asked for, but I can remember writing that list and you didn't have any of the character flaws.

It is amazing how we have changed. You were shy (at least I thought you were, but perhaps you weren't really, and I carried on giving you that label). You were always funny, very funny and I really appreciate that; it makes for a good, happy life if you can have a laugh together.

Your confidence has grown, and the things you have achieved are incredible. I admire everything that you have done, and I am so proud of you as a husband and as Beth and Mike's father.

I appreciate that you have been an emotional crutch for me over the years when I've gone through very tough times, and you have helped me to get through them. It's only because of your love and respect for me that I have conquered my demons. You helped me to become more courageous, hard-working and positive in outlook.

We're going through another cycle in our lives now and starting a new venture. I know we'll be successful with our new venture and everything will work out fine. 'If you conceive it, believe it and you will receive it.' That little saying was true when I wrote my list for the husband I wanted all those years ago, so I know it works. Be the person you want to be as we go on to the next chapter of our lives together. Do what you want, knowing that I love you very much and will support you in everything that you really want in life.

I do feel very blessed that we are together and I hope you do too.

Thank you for great sex.

Thank you for my cup of tea every morning.

Thank you for your smile when I return from anywhere.

Thank you for the dinners you cook.

Thank you for tidying kitchen and emptying the dishwasher every day.

Thank you for making me feel special.

Thank you for letting me be me.

Thank you for telling me the truth.

Thank you for your wisdom and advice.

Thank you for loving me.

Thank you for being a wonderful dad to Beth and Mike and a devoted grandfather to Scarlett and Jas. I think that shows what sort of person you are where Scarlett and Jas are concerned. They absolutely love you to bits for being you. It is funny how they don't leave you alone and want you to do everything for them – a testament of their love for you. They can't get enough of you but it's true, unconditional love. They love you for being you. I hope you love yourself as much as everybody loves you. You are perfect!

    All my love, always –

Julie xxx

That all said, I'm still writing letters in my local media as I become older and wiser!

Dear Editor,

    In and around Tenbury Wells is a fantastic place for a daily walk, particularly in the summer. Walking for me is the finest form of exercise, and when with Julie, my wife, it is a great opportunity for a talk and walk. During our latest and favourite walk through Saint Michael's, we entered Oldwood. I exchanged niceties with the fishmonger. A little further up, I passed the baker's house. Stepping out, I waved to the police officer just as the fire fighter was leaving his house. We then passed the farmer and the author's house, the solicitor and clockmaker. Just before we rounded the corner, I shouted across to the vicar to 'say one for me!' We passed the accountant's and the organist's, the doctor's, the vet's house and church warden's and the teacher's house as well as the nurse's. Walking further, we waved to the councillor and then the architect. With a population of three hundred, you would think there would be a candlestick maker!

Cliff Slade
Tenbury Wells

Maybe a topic or event isn't to our liking; I always try to respect other people's enjoyment and maybe give a different perspective or a philosophical outlook. This letter was printed in relation to some big road closures and disruption that affected many people, and the uproar and complaints were tangible!

Dear Sir,

Cllr Ken Pollock (W.N. Thursday, October 19th) has wisely noted that many individuals and businesses are against the return of the proposed 'Velo' cycle event to our Worcestershire roads in 2018. I operate a transport-related business which, just by its definition, depends on the unhindered use of our road network. I am a realist and not idealist and accept, at times, that this, for many reasons, is not possible, and I plan accordingly. The 2017 'Velo' event did have an impact on me personally, and I had to change my business planned route, at a cost to me. As I observed the event through gritted teeth, I have to concede it really was a spectacle whereupon professional, amateur and newbie cyclists of all ages were enjoying the cycling on open, safe, and restricted roads whilst apparently raising funds for their chosen charity. Spectators and families were also on mass, enjoying the outside event, and I noted a little girl holding a sign saying 'keep going Daddy'!

I am not a great cycle lover, albeit I did enjoy my chopper bike in the 1970s! However, I also appreciate cycling for many is a love and passion and keeps them fit and healthy. Cllr Pollock also recognises that some people will gain whilst other people and businesses may lose, and says that this will be well debated, taking on board the many views and experiences from the 2017 event. Good luck to him on that! I am now going to select the winning lottery numbers for the weekend, which is much easier.

Cliff Slade
Tenbury Wells

From time to time, we all have little commotions in our community, and in Tenbury we had a water shortage which was an inconvenience but worthy of a letter of thanks, mixed with a little bit of sentiment and humour.

Dear Sir,

As a WR15 resident, and like others, I would have preferred the Severn Trent water drama that left Tenbury without water for three days not to have happened. However, the rapid organisation, information and updates that Tenbury received from Severn Trent was nothing short of absolutely brilliant. Bottled water was being delivered to the vulnerable and key points such as the hospital, doctors and schools. We also had two well-organised flowing collection points established, each side of the river, at the swimming pool, and hospital car parks. These collection points were staffed by polite, helpful and well-informed volunteers with the Red Cross and Salvation Army also swinging into action where every situation and eventuality was covered.

It was also great to see our town councillors manning the pumps and out delivering. For my part, I collected as much water as I could from one point and then drove around to the other collection point and filled up again! I duplicated this for most of the three days and now have 2601 litres of water, or three hundred and twenty-five cases, or four and a half pallets! I learnt this method of 'I'm alright Jack' in 1974 when I quickly purchased most of the sugar

available due to the global sugar shortage.
I still have many 2lb bags of 'Silver Spoon'
sugar now which is great. Similarly, I also
have in the freezer many 'Mothers Pride' medium sliced loaves of bread from the bread
shortage in the same year! I noticed during
our local water shortage that other people
were also copying my technique.

Cliff Slade
Tenbury Wells

There is always something to think about and write
about; I just write when I feel a muse coming on!

Dear Sir,
    'Big up the bugs'.
    At school in the 1960s and 1970s, school
dinners were always cooked on site and absolutely delicious. More often than not, both
at school and at home, it was common to find
a cooked or uncooked slug, fly, or another
unidentified bug which would make me squirm
and retch.
    To date, on our weekly shopping expedi-
tion, I now purposely look for any such in-
sects and creepy crawlies typically found
within the organic area as an indication of
the products' quality and chemical-free condition.
    I am lucky to have an organic box of
fruit and vegetables delivered to our door-
step every week, which is packed with a random selection of commodities. As it is my

task to prepare the vegetables for dinner, in particular on Sunday, when our three grandchildren dine with us, I observed a slug attached to my cauliflower, little unknown mites on our cabbage, and what I can only describe as some form of grub burrowed deeply within our spuds. These days it really makes me feel good that finding these little arthropods and organisms highlight the fact that I, and my ever-extending family, are eating fresh, insecticide- and pesticide-free food.

I am fully aware that cost matters for both me as a consumer, and the need for ours, and the world's farming community, to mass produce on an industrial scale to feed the masses and requires positive or negative bug control.

That aside, we then have to consider the footprint, environment, and how eco-friendly my cauli is. Crikey! This is all too much for me. Now, where did I put my glass of sulphated, pesticide-ridden, and high-sugared bottle of red wine?

Cliff Slade
Tenbury Wells

With putting my letters into a book, the next letter gently introduces my plan and announces my book intention!

Dear Sir,

Very rarely do I write a letter to the Advertiser. Walking around Tenbury, individuals regularly comment, 'you haven't a letter in the Advertiser this week', and then ask if I am OK!

If ever I pen a letter I have to be inspired or feel Tenbury needs representing or has been unjustly debased. I may even say 'thank you' to an organisation or individual for providing something or representing this great place we live in! I sometimes wonder if people think that writing a load of rubbish and nonsense is easy and straight forward; well it's not – it takes a lot of effort and thought to regularly produce babble, gibberish, mumble jumble drivel. That said, I am in a state of scripter stagnancy at the moment. I think us professional, creative authors refer to this state as 'writer's block'!

One day I will surprise those Tenbury folk not converted to my insignificant musings and write a sophisticated, bestselling book, you see!

Cliff Slade
Tenbury Wells

Why have I taken the time to write this book and expose myself, personally and emotionally, from behind the pen?

Can we change or not change the destination of our character from birth, from our parents, from our learnt behaviour, from our environment? We are animals at birth and have one instinctive aim – survival. My parents or in my case, parent, then fed me, protected me, kept me warm, and I instinctively knew where and what family I belonged to, and my character and emotions then moved through stages and developed accordingly. The security of that unit was compromised as my family situation dramatically changed, and so did I. My trust and the sanctuary that was my mother and home affected my self-esteem and self-worth in a positive and negative way. Ironically, those experiences allowed or forced me to introvert and introspect with positive and life-changing thoughts, actions and events that defined my ever-shifting, emotional journey. My only emotional shortfall was love and intimacy. All other emotions were successfully hard-wired into my being and therefore I graduated through life stages, not only successfully, but with merit, although love and intimacy are pretty big tools to be short of in my toolbox of life.

I write better than I speak or act, so writing this has been a vehicle to express my love, and if the reader, and particularly my close family feel the love, then I have had some intimacy with you and them. I have always had the ability to laugh at myself and I never cease to be amused. Therefore, it necessarily follows that before I can love others, firstly, I have to love myself. C. S. Lewis said, 'you can't go back and change the beginning, but you can start where you are and change the ending', and that is the very reason for writing this book in letters.

Initially, I was the youngest of three children until my half-sister was born, Judith. Judith sadly passed away in 1998, so all through my life I have had two siblings, my sister, Pauline, who was the eldest, and my brother, Glenn, who was the middle child. We are all close, albeit we have all had our moments. That's what brothers and sisters do, although I do struggle to remember a time where I have fallen out with either of them. I have purposely, throughout this book of letters, left them out and used the pronoun 'I'. We are all close, but although they lived their lives with me, I cannot, and would not contemplate using the word 'we' because I cannot possibly speak or make a judgement on their behalf; their thoughts and subsequent judgements belong to them alone. One thing that is a fact and very strange, is that we all came from the same broken family, broken as in my mum was married three times. Statistically, it is a fact that adults whose parents divorced have a greater chance of their relationship failing. Pauline is in her forty second year of marriage, Glenn is in his thirty fourth year, and I am in my thirty fifth year. How strange! Although my sister, Pauline, who is married to Geoffrey never had children, my brother Glenn and his wife Angie had two children, Carl and

Katie. Carl and Katie were first cousins to Beth and Mike and they were always close and together at birthdays and special occasions.

Glenn and Angie unfortunately lost Kate and the shock, tragedy and upset at that time was immense, and the emotional consequences of that awful day still live with us all. Kate is greatly missed, and I could not comprehend losing a child, or even try to feel the way Glenn and Angie and Carl felt then and now.

I have written this letter that is now a book. It has been very easy to write this letter, but it has been difficult to know what to include and who to include, as well as who to leave out and what to leave out. I have not included some wild things that I have done and different people I have befriended, met or worked with because I will have nothing to smile about when I am old. So, that is it, really. My emotions, sentiments and feelings are yet again changing.

I didn't ever believe that I could love anyone more than my own children until my little grandchildren arrived, Scarlett aged six, Jasmine aged four and Hugo aged seven months!

So that is just a little bit of me behind and beyond and behind the letters and in letters.

In the meantime, I'll keep writing letters for one reason or another, but there is always a meaning, message or a feeling behind someone, who for some reason, has penned a letter.

I will finish where I started, with that framed poem on my wall that I pass every day, with my modern-day thought that has determined my being.

Princes & Kings.

How odd life is, that irrespective of our class or status in life, we are all given the same opportunities and strive to construct this time without end?

We are all working under the same timepiece and adhering to the same regulations and set of laws. We are all born with the means to develop our own destiny. Whether it is judged as moving forwards or backwards, only we will know at that time when we are called away from this sublunary abode.

Cliff Slade